TECHNOLOGY PLAY AND BRAIN DEVELOPMENT

Technology Play and Brain Development brings together current research on play development, learning technology, and brain development. The authors first navigate the play technology and brain development interface, highlighting the interactive qualities that make up each component. Next, they survey the changes in play materials and the variations in time periods for play that have occurred over the past 15-20 years, and then explain how these changes have had the potential to affect this play/brain developmental interaction. The authors also cover various types of technology-augmented play materials used by children at age levels from infancy to adolescence, and describe the particular qualities that may enhance or change brain development. In so doing, they present information on previous and current studies of the play and technology interface, in addition to providing behavioral data collected from parents and children of varied ages related to their play with different types of play materials. Significantly, they discuss how such play may affect social, emotional, moral, and cognitive development, and review futurist predictions about the potential qualities of human behavior needed by generations to come. The authors conclude with advice to toy and game designers, parents, educators, and the wider community on ways to enhance the quality of technology-augmented play experiences so that play will continue to promote the development of human characteristics needed in the future.

Doris Bergen is Distinguished Professor Emerita at Miami University. Her research focuses on play theory, humor development, effects of technology-augmented play, and ERP effects during videogame play. As a child she preferred play with blocks, making "small worlds," and now she enjoys using her spatial skills to take down iPad block tower structures.

Darrel R. Davis is an Associate Professor at Miami University. His research interests include the effects of technology-related play and the use of technology in diverse educational settings. As a child he loved to play with action figures and toy vehicles and now prefers outdoor activities and participating in team sports.

Jason T. Abbitt is an Associate Professor at Miami University. He is an educator and researcher focused on helping educators use technology for teaching and learning. His favorite forms of play involve building and tinkering, from his use of Legos and Erector sets as a child to a focus on coding and microcontrollers today.

TECHNOLOGY PLAY AND BRAIN DEVELOPMENT

Infancy to Adolescence and Future Implications

*Doris Bergen, Darrel R. Davis,
and Jason T. Abbitt*

Routledge
Taylor & Francis Group

NEW YORK AND LONDON

First published 2016
by Routledge
711 Third Avenue, New York, NY 10017

and by Routledge
2 Park Square, Milton Park, Abingdon, Oxon OX14 4RN

Routledge is an imprint of the Taylor & Francis Group, an informa business

© 2016 Taylor & Francis

The right of Doris Bergen, Darrel R. Davis, and Jason T. Abbitt to be
identified as authors of this work has been asserted by them in accordance
with sections 77 and 78 of the Copyright, Designs and Patents Act 1988.

All rights reserved. No part of this book may be reprinted or reproduced or
utilised in any form or by any electronic, mechanical, or other means, now
known or hereafter invented, including photocopying and recording, or in
any information storage or retrieval system, without permission in writing
from the publishers.

Trademark notice: Product or corporate names may be trademarks or registered
trademarks, and are used only for identification and explanation without
intent to infringe.

Library of Congress Cataloging-in-Publication Data
Bergen, Doris.
  Technology play and brain development : implications for the future of
human behaviors / Doris Bergen, Darrel Davis, Jason Abbitt.
     pages cm
  Includes bibliographical references and index.
  1. Social psychology. 2. Human behavior. 3. Technology. I. Davis,
Darrel (Darrel R.) II. Abbitt, Jason. III. Title.
  BF698.95.B475 2016
  155.4'13—dc23
  2015005375

ISBN: 978-1-848-72476-1 (hbk)
ISBN: 978-1-848-72477-8 (pbk)
ISBN: 978-1-315-68143-6 (ebk)

Typeset in Bembo
by Apex CoVantage, LLC

To the playful humans who enabled us not only to survive but also to flourish in past centuries and to the playful humans who will lead us into a future of expanded human possibilities.

CONTENTS

ACKNOWLEDGMENT

Our thanks to the parents and children who described the types of play that they enjoyed and shared their views on the value of both traditional and technology-augmented play experiences.

INTRODUCTION

The Importance of Understanding the Brain/Play/Technology Interface

The authors of this book have approached the topic of effects of technology on brain maturation and social, emotional, moral, and cognitive development from varied perspectives, but they are in agreement that stakeholders, including parents, educators, psychologists, technology designers and implementers, as well as the greater community, should be collaborating to ensure that the technology-augmented play experiences of today's children and adolescents are well designed in order to facilitate growth and development that will give them the versatility and the resilience that they will need to meet future events. Presently, opinions on effects of intensive technology-rich environments on child and adolescent development and learning are varied and not always supported by research evidence.

The first author, Bergen, has discussed issues related to the potential effects of technology-augmented toys on young children's play for over a decade and conducted research on young children's play with such toys. With colleagues, she also has initiated a study of brain wave responses to video game play and written theoretical pieces speculating on effects of varied types of technology play on brain development. With co-author Davis, she also has explored the role child and adolescent play with real and virtual playthings may have on moral development. Davis has further explored the types of video and online play that college students report. Abbitt has studied effects of technology-enhanced learning materials in various educational contexts and, with Davis, has presented work on the effects of instructor texting to improve student learning. Thus, the impetus for this book has come from the authors' belief that it is important to address the interface between technology-augmented play and brain maturation, as well as other developmental areas, and to examine factors that might influence this interface both positively and negatively.

Research into the effects of technology-augmented play is controversial, with a number of writers pointing with alarm to the possibilities of harm from early and consistent exposure to technology-augmented toys and media, while other writers have described how these media can enhance human learning if designed and used appropriately. There has been scholarly work that has addressed both particular concerns and possibilities, but there has been no book that has comprehensively discussed the play/brain/technology interface issues addressed in this book. It is likely that technology-augmented play will have both positive and negative effects on brain maturation processes, especially if children and adolescents have extensive and long-term exposure to such play materials. Perhaps such exposure may differentially affect not only brain development but also the social, emotional, moral, and cognitive aspects of many other human behaviors. These changes may be useful and relevant at a future time and assist humans to adapt to future conditions or they may cause humans to lose abilities and skills that continue to remain relevant and essential for human life. Thus, the authors believe that a book that brings together current research knowledge on such developmental factors and explains how they may interface with the representation modes and affordances of various technology-based play materials has been needed to provide scholars and students with a perspective for further systematic research.

Scope and Sequence

Chapter 1 discusses how both play and brain development have nonlinear dynamic systems qualities, and describes the processes by which play development occurs and interfaces with brain maturation. It presents the theoretical view that cognitive understanding proceeds through enactive (motoric action with objects), iconic (linking perceptual images of objects), and symbolic (using language and other symbols to represent objects) levels (Bruner, 1964); discusses potential social, emotional, moral, and cognitive issues that play supports; defines technology; describes the nonlinear dynamic qualities of technology; and suggests how such qualities may interface with play and brain development. Chapter 2 describes the historical role of technology in the design of play materials and the changes in play environments that have occurred with the advent of technology-augmented play materials. It also reviews both a number of writers' perspectives on the potential positive and negative effects of this change in the play environment and evidence of such changes in play experiences drawn from research on adults' memories of their own play. The authors also describe the theoretical lens of "affordance" theory (Gibson, 1969, Carr, 2000) and "modes of representation" (Bruner, 1964). Further, the concepts of physical and virtual "contexts" (Milgram & Kishino, 1994) are used to analyze potential effects. Chapter 3 describes the various types of technology-augmented play materials presently being used by young persons from infancy to adolescence. It describes these affordances and contexts and suggests ways that physical and virtual technology contexts may have different affordances and contexts, which may result in varied effects on child and adolescent development. Chapter 4 describes the authors' research on young children's initial interactions with technology-augmented toys and video game play. It also presents the opinions of a group of parents, children, and adolescents about past play experiences and present day technology-augmented play. Their views of advantages and disadvantages of such play and its possible effect on various developmental areas are shared. Chapter 5 addresses speculations from futurists regarding the types of skills that humans will need in future life periods and examines those possibilities in relation to the skills that may be promoted by various types of technology-augmented play. The potential changes in human brain development and behavior that may occur due to the changes in play behaviors are described and evaluated. In Chapter 6 the authors provide suggestions for parents, educators and psychologists, technology toy manufacturers, digital game makers, online play designers, and community stakeholders that may promote healthy and future-enhancing brain development as children and adolescents engage in play with technology-augmented as well as traditional play materials.

The authors believe, as Emily Dickinson reminds us, that the brain is an amazing organ that defines us and our world. Thus, its fate in the future must be considered in a technology-augmented world.

> The Brain—is wider than the Sky—
> For—put them side by side—
> The one the other will contain
> With ease—and You—beside—
>
> The Brain is deeper than the sea—
> For—hold them—Blue to Blue—
> The one the other will absorb—
> As Sponges—Buckets—do—
>
> The Brain is just the weight of God—
> For—Heft them—Pound for Pound—
> And they will differ—if they do—
> As Syllable from Sound—

Reprinted by permission from Johnson, T.H. *The complete poems of Emily Dickinson* (1955), New York: Little Brown & Co.

References

Bruner, J.S. (1964). The course of cognitive growth. *American Psychologist, 19*(1), 1–15.

Carr, M. (2000). Technological affordances, social practice and learning narratives in an early childhood setting. *International Journal of Technology and Design Education, 10*, 61–79.

Gibson, E.J. (1969). *Principles of perceptual learning and development.* New York: Appleton-Century-Crofts.

Milgram, P., & Kishino, F. (1994). *A taxonomy of mixed reality visual displays. IEICE TRANS-ACTIONS on Information and Systems,* 77(12), 1321–1329.

1

BRAIN MATURATION AND TYPICAL PLAY DEVELOPMENT FROM INFANCY THROUGH ADOLESCENCE

Complimentary Dynamic Processes with Technology

The plane from San Francisco to Atlanta was crowded, with every seat filled. Tina (age 3½) was seated in the middle of a three-seat row, with her dad in the window seat and an older adult in the aisle seat. While the plane was boarding and taxiing for takeoff, Tina was talkative and wiggly and it seemed like this long flight would be very tedious for her. While her dad was getting her settled, she kept pointing to his iPad™, which he had put in the seat pocket and he reminded Tina a number of times that she would have to wait to get that until after the plane was in the air. Once the plane was on the way, he pulled out two little pink ear buds and put them in Tina's ears and then put the iPad on a Disney movie. Tina sat quietly in her seat absorbed in the movie for most of the rest of the trip. She did eat a snack and, during the last half hour of the trip, she dozed off. However, the iPad movie engaged her attention for over 2 hours! Her dad had very little talk with his daughter after the iPad took over.

Studies of the dynamic relationship among brain developmental processes, child and adolescent play experiences, and the influences of technology-augmented play materials are only in initial stages. However, it is likely that play development and brain development may be differentially affected by play with technology-augmented materials. What brain development effects will occur due to humans' pervasive interactions with technologically advanced materials is not a new question, however, as various theorists and researchers have speculated on it in the past.

For example, in pondering the course of cognitive growth and the reasons for the human evolution of large brains, Bruner (1964) drew attention to a paper written on the one hundredth anniversary of Darwin's (1859) publication of *The Origin of the Species* in which the authors asserted that the brain's development has occurred because of the "result of a technical-social life" (Washburn & Howell, 1960, p. 49).

Bruner proposed that intellectual functioning has always been driven by "a series of technological advances in the use of mind" (p. 1), which enabled humans to manage in increasingly complex environments and "construct models of their world" (ibid.). He hypothesized that over the long evolutionary period, humans have increased their intellectual power by learning to use and understand three types of technological artifacts: amplifiers of human motor capabilities (e.g., wheels, bicycles), amplifiers of sensory capacities (e.g., radios, magnets), and amplifiers of human ratiocinative capacities (e.g., language and other symbol systems)—all of which are transmitted by the culture in which humans live. Each of these has a "mode of representation" (p. 2). *Enactive* representation occurs through motor responses, which are the earliest mode of understanding. For example, young children's tricycle riding or block building involves motoric interactions with the environment and encodes knowledge in the muscles, and this knowledge can then be applied to other actions in the environment. *Iconic* representations involve the organization of images or models and the understanding that such pictures or images of perceptual events can "stand for" the actual environmental features. This is evident when a young child can point to a picture of "shoe" or "kitten" or find the "truck" or the "car" in a storybook. *Symbolic* representation begins when children can use an arbitrary symbol system such as language or numbers to encode meaning. This occurs when a child knows the symbol "Bill" stands for his name or can point to the symbol "3" to show how old he is. Once these modes of representation are learned, humans can produce combinations of images or actions that go beyond "real-world" experiences. In Bruner's view, this ability to "become specialized by the use of technological implements" (p. 2) has made the evolution of human abilities possible. If new technological artifacts give humans different interactive experiences, then future evolution of the human species through interaction with present day and future technologies is a definite possibility.

Views of the Play/Brain Relationship

The role playfulness may serve in fostering human brain and cognitive development has been of interest to various theorists such as Plato, who in his book of *Laws* (360 BC) suggested that children's play (*paidia*) had significance as a venue for learning and developing basic habits of character (*paideia*) (see Morris, 1998). At later time periods, the view that children's playful activity has educational and developmental meaning was emphasized by many theorists, including Comenius (1632, 1657), Rousseau (1792/1911), Froebel (1887), Dewey (1910, 1916), and Hall, (1920, 1924). In the mid-20th century, Huizinga (1950) wrote that playfulness is an integral behavior of the human species and thus he called humans *Homo Ludens* ("man, the player"). Huizinga's view of the evolutionary importance of play was also discussed by Ellis (1998), who asserted that playful behaviors positively influence the ability of biological systems to exhibit rapid adaptation when unpredictable events that threaten survival are encountered. Human existence has always been precarious and he suggests it is likely that humans who had the greatest range of adaptive behaviors to meet changing environmental or social conditions (i.e., the most playful humans) were the ones who were most likely to survive. In his view, that is why and how present humans have inherited their intensely playful qualities.

Researchers who have studied play in animals also have lent insights into possible play-brain connections. For example, Lorenz (1971) indicated that, for many animal species, the curiosity young animals exhibit in their play is a characteristic needed for expressing new behaviors in varied settings. He compared the play of children to the research of adult scientists. Fagen (1981), who wrote extensively about animal play, agreed, stating that such play is essentially "a biological adaptation for producing novel behaviors" (p. 36). Recently, researchers using brain imaging techniques with animals have studied how the "playful brain" evolved in both animal and human species. (Iwaniuk et al., 2001; Pellis & Iwaniuk, 2004). Their research shows that animals with larger brains compared to their body size also exhibit the most playfulness. Relevant to the question of technology-augmented play effects, Whiting and Pope Edwards (1988), after conducting cross-cultural studies of children's play, concluded that the types of play in which children engage are malleable due to social and cultural messages, thus reflecting the cultural meanings of the society in which it occurs. If this is the case, then the present day cultural messages promoted through technology-augmented play may make this the preferred type of play for young humans in the 21st century. Freysinger (2006), in discussing play throughout the life span, states that the types of human play that are exhibited are "situated in a specific historical time and the economic, political, religious, and social reality of the day" (p. 60). In a recent discussion of cultural neuroscience theory, Kitayama (2013) has explained that, because of the brain's neuroplasticity, brain activity patterns may differ when varied culturally sanctioned behaviors are elicited. Thus, it is possible that the play behaviors promoted in a technologically pervasive culture will have a lasting impact on children's brain structures and functions.

Although they did not tie play behaviors to specific areas of the brain, two prominent theorists who did describe specific developmental relationships between various types of play and cognitive growth are Piaget (1945, 1965) and Vygotsky (1962, 1967). From observations of his own children's play in infancy and his study of older boys' marble game play, Piaget closely linked the various stages of play development to the growth of cognitive and moral abilities. His view was that children used play to construct their knowledge of the world by trying to relate their new experiences to their existing cognitive schema and their developing thought processes. Vygotsky investigated ways that children's play fostered learning of their cultural language and he stated that, especially when children engage in pretend play, their spontaneous concept development is fostered, leading to growth in self-regulation and development of internal modes of thought.

These earlier perspectives on the potential role of play in affecting brain maturation and the development of human capabilities provide the background for present investigations, because, if, as these theorists have asserted, human survival skills, cultural meanings, and cognitive advancement are all linked to playful behaviors, then the types of play in which children and adolescents are engaging at the present time are likely to affect their cognitive and social-emotional development, their adaptability to meet cultural demands, and even their survival in the world of the future. That is why the question of how the changing play environment may both positively and negatively affect brain development and subsequent behavior adaptability for children and adolescents is of interest, as is the question of the potential effects of such technology-augmented play on the broader society of the future. Because the brain maturation process provides many opportunities for environmental affordances such as play materials and technological artifacts to affect the nature of the adult brain, it is important to understand the brain maturation process (Bergen & Coscia, 2001). A glossary with a list of definitional terms related to the brain and diagrams of basic brain and nervous system areas are included in the appendix.

Brain Maturation during the Child and Adolescent Years

In the late 20th and early 21st century, information regarding how the brains of humans and other creatures operate has grown exponentially, due to the invention of research techniques that can observe both the electrical and chemical processes occurring in the brain at various ages as well as the expansion of synaptic connections and subsequent pruning of neuronal structures from birth to adulthood. Because over 71% of human brain development occurs after birth and brain maturation continues until about age 20, the experiences children and adolescents have (including their play experiences!) profoundly affect the ways their individual brains are structured and, consequentially, the ways they will perform throughout the rest of life. Researchers have found some differences in the adult brains of various individuals who have pursued certain careers. While the brain does retain some plasticity throughout life and later experiences may affect brain structures and functions, there is no question that the experiences of the first

20 years of life have the greatest impact in determining which areas of the brain are more densely formed and activated and which areas are pruned more precisely before the brain reaches its mature state. The consensus of researchers is that both individual genetic and experiential factors are crucial in determining brain structure and function in adulthood. As the Hindu phase "Sarvam annam" reminds us, for the developing human brain, "everything is food."

Infant Brain Maturation

The sequence of brain development in infants and young children has been well charted by researchers during the past 20 years. At birth, the neonate already has about 100 billion neurons, which were created during the prenatal stage. The neuron has three major parts, a cell body, dendrites that receive information, and axons that transmit information. These neurons compose the majority of those that the individual will have throughout life, but many of them are not yet connected in neural networks. Only those needed for essential life processes are connected firmly at birth so the process of synaptogenesis (creating neuronal network connections) is of great importance during the first few years of life. If the brain is well nourished and adequately stimulated, each neuron can produce up to 15,000 synapses (Lezak et al. 2004) during early development. The brain's weight increases from about 1 pound at birth to 2 pounds by 1 year, partly due to the increase in synapses and partly due to the coating of nerve axons with fatty glial cells (myelination), which act to speed neural signals. Research has shown that the brain stem and cerebellum begin myelination first, before the cerebral areas, and that myelination of the frontal lobes continues into adolescence.

The occipital (visual) lobe of the cortex is one of the first parts of the brain that has rapid synaptic growth and, therefore, this is one of the first areas in which pruning (the loss of nonessential connections) takes place. This is why treatment for young children with vision difficulties usually takes place at an early age before the pruning process in the visual cortex is highly active. Synaptogenesis also is especially active during the first years in the parietal lobe of the cortex (motor and sensory brain areas), and this synaptic growth is clearly seen in the increasing sensory and motor behavioral skills that children develop in the first years of life enabling them to demonstrate "enactive" cognition.

Social development is promoted by the activation of "mirror neurons," located in the premotor cortex, which connects portions of the parietal lobe with the occipital lobe and various other areas in the cortical regions (Rizzolatti & Craighero, 2004). The function of these neurons seems to be to enable infants to transform visual information into understanding of the actions of others by engaging them in the imitation of the observed behavioral acts. This infant understanding usually occurs first in interaction with parents or others in their social world, but young children's understanding of the actions of objects (e.g., toys) also seems to be derived from this mirror neuron system (Bergen & Woodin, 2010). In Bruner's terms, this ability also may be related to the "enactive" mode of thought. When the infant is about 6 months old, synaptogenesis also begins to increase between the limbic system, which contains the autonomic and emotion centers, and the frontal lobe of the cortex, which involves higher thinking processes. Although young infants have many emotional reactions, their ability to understand and label these emotions is not well developed until the synaptic connections between the limbic system and the cortex increase. When these connections are more strongly established during the toddler and preschool years, children can begin to use "iconic" and "symbolic" levels of thought.

Childhood Brain Maturation

The toddler years are a time of great brain activity because synaptogenesis expansion is greatest at that time, and by age 3 the child's brain has about 1,000 trillion connections, which is twice the density of the adult brain (Shore, 1997). The toddler brain is about two and a half times as active as the adult brain because it is not as efficient as the adult brain. The weight of the brain continues to increase due to the rapid expansion of synapses and the myelination of the axons and by the age of 6, the child's brain has about 90% of its adult weight. Synaptogenesis in the frontal lobe is most prominent during the latter part of early childhood, and the frontal lobe has the greatest synaptic density at about age 7. Because pruning of each area begins when synaptic density reaches its highest point, pruning in the frontal lobe begins in earnest in middle and later childhood. Pruning results in greater efficiency and thus, from age 3 to 8, children's speed of processing, memory activity, and problem-solving skills are increasing. The P300 wave, which is related to attention, problem-solving abilities, and speed of processing, begins to be observed at about age 7 (Eliot, 1999). Thus, less brain energy (glucose) is burned as the brain becomes more efficient (Haier, 1993). During this 3–8 age period individualization of the brain also becomes more evident as the structures and functions interact with environmental experiences. According to Eliot (1999), "once a given brain region has passed the refinement stage, its critical period has ended, and the opportunity to rewire it is significantly limited" (p. 38).

During the later elementary age period (8–12), the brain continues to mature, especially in the frontal lobe areas. For example, the dorso-lateral prefrontal cortex, which is involved in monitoring executive functioning skills, is made more efficient through pruning nonessential neural connections (Bauer et al., 2010). The neural circuits that an individual has used less frequently are the ones most likely to be pruned and, although such pruning increases speed of processing, the pruning also results in less flexibility to restructure brain areas. This process of individualization of brain structures is often apparent in the narrowing of activity and learning choices that children make in late elementary and middle childhood (Bergen & Coscia, 2001). During this period the brain increases its ability to use "iconic" and "symbolic" methods of representing thought.

Adolescent Brain Maturation

Recent research on the adolescent brain has discovered how much more brain maturation is still occurring during the years from 12 to 20. During middle childhood (12–14) young adolescents still use a larger area of the brain than adults do to carry out discrimination tasks because the maturation of the frontal lobe is still occurring. Myelination continues, glucose use declines, and pruning is extensive. By middle childhood, there is evidence of stable brain differences; however, areas related to executive functioning are still not mature. Research comparing adolescent and adult parietal, temporal, and occipital areas of the brain show that they are relatively similar, which indicates that those brain areas have reached a relatively mature state. In contrast, adolescent frontal lobes, which are the site of executive functioning skills, are not as mature as those of adults. All three of the thought systems described by Bruner (i.e., enactive, iconic, and symbolic) are well established, however. Although the adolescent has more advanced thinking and reasoning skills, there is still much development occurring and "the implication of these changes are not well established" (Bronk, 2010, p. 49). During adolescence another area of the brain is still maturing. That is the limbic system, which is involved in learning, memory, and emotions. For example, the adolescent brain shows continuing maturation of the amygdala, which perceives and interprets emotions; the insula, which is involved in emotions and risk-taking decisions and behaviors; and the hippocampus, which is involved in emotional, learning, and memory reactivity (Baird et al., 1999).

Longitudinal studies of brain development from childhood to adulthood show that the volume of gray matter (involved in synaptogenesis and pruning) increases and decreases in various areas of the brain in relation to the maturation of those areas, but that the volume of white matter (the myelin coatings) continues to increase until the third decade of life (Giedd & Rapoport, 2010). These researchers noted that female brains appear to reach peak periods of maturation slightly earlier than male brains, and hormonal changes in males and females also have been shown to affect brain functioning, especially in the limbic and frontal lobe areas. In a comparison of 12–16 year olds and 23–30 year olds, Sowell et al. (1999) concluded that the reported reduction in gray matter (connective tissue) occurring between adolescence and adulthood was a reflection of myelination that still was continuing after the teen years in peripheral regions of the cortex, which improved cognitive functioning into adulthood. Because brain maturation is a long process that is not fully completed until early adulthood, the play experiences of adolescents continue to be an important influence.

Play Development in the Child and Adolescent Years

According to theorists and researchers who have studied how play develops, the most common type of play seen in infancy, usually called *practice* play, involves repeating activities with increasing elaboration or difficulty and this type of play is very evident in the first year of life. Typically, infants and young children first will try to see what a particular object does when they interact with it, but soon they begin to play with the object; that is, they try to find many ways to interact with the object. As Hutt (1971) states, first children find out what an object does and then they explore what they can do with the object. She calls the first activity "exploration" and the second "play." Practice play is one way that Bruner's "enac-tive" mode of cognition is demonstrated. Social practice play also occurs in infant interaction with parents, siblings, and other individuals in a kind of "turn-taking" model. A good example of this is the "peek-a-boo" play routine that engages child and adult, and, although initially initiated by the adult, it is quickly taken over by the child, who controls the "peeks," with increasingly great laughter. Rep-etition with elaboration occurs not only with people and objects but also with language and musical sounds, and provides increasingly child-controlled playful interactions.

By the end of the first year of life, usually with an initial demonstration by adult or older child, *pretense* begins. Young children begin to act "as if" in their play by pretending that objects have social meanings and engaging in short social scripts. For example, "drinking" milk from an empty cup, "feeding" a doll with imaginary food, or "talking" on the phone are often the first evidences of such pretense. In relation to Bruner's cognitive schema, being able to treat appropri-ately a replica object as a real object (e.g., use driving motions with a plastic or wooden "car" or hugging a doll "baby") is an early example of the "iconic" mode of cognition. In pretense the "play frame" (Bateson, 1956) is understood even by young children and they begin to demonstrate their ability to respond to a lan-guage label or action demonstration that shows the symbolic meaning given to the objects used in the play. When the language label itself prompts a particular action, for example, acting the role of "mommy" or "doctor," in Bruner's terms, they are now able to demonstrate a "symbolic" mode of cognition. Pretense becomes increasingly elaborated over the next 5 years, and it is often observed as the major play mode of children during the toddler and preschool years. Elabo-rated pretense involves child-controlled scripts, roles, and scenes, both reality and fantasy based. Children use whatever experiential material is available, drawing on their life experiences or from books, television, and other media. Vygotsky (1967) has explained how the elaborated scripts that are used in pretense chal-lenge children to act in roles that require varied social skills that may be above their present level of development and thus such pretense promotes both cogni-tive and social development.

In the elementary-age period, pretense continues to be a major play mode but is not as obvious to observers since it often involves small-scale dolls or action figures, elaborated but private settings, and detailed scripts that may take many days to be played out. In studies of adults' memories of their childhood play, adults often report examples of this type of pretense, which involves constructing the design of the "set" in which the pretense will occur (Bergen, 2009). Such "small-worlds" play has been reported by many McArthur Fellows as a major play mode of their youth (Root-Bernstein & Root-Bernstein, 2006). This set building is a mature form of *construction*, which involves play with building materials such as blocks and replica small-scale objects (e g., toy animals, figures, trucks). This type of play becomes prominent during the preschool age period. The difference between such construction play and actual construction is that the playfulness in the act of constructing is important (Forman, 2006). In contrast to construction that is made to last, in playful construction the designs change constantly and, once built, these constructions are as easily destroyed by the children in order to build another different world with the same materials. Children experiment with objects and other materials to learn more about the laws that operate in the physical world, and their constructions have dynamic system qualities. Pretense is often combined with construction play; that is, the "set" is designed in which the pretense occurs.

According to Piaget, the ability to play *games-with-rules* requires other sets of skills that involve social, cognitive, and moral decision making. Usually older toddlers can play one-rule games such as peek-a-boo or hide and find, but the elaboration period for games with rules begins in later preschool and becomes a major type of play during the elementary-age years. Most early games have only one or two rules and these rules can change often, depending on the players' skills and interests. Games with rules are evident in board games and in the type of outdoor games of the "child culture" that have been cataloged by researchers (Opie & Opie, 1969). The difference between such games and activities called "sports" is that games with rules are controlled by children and involve adapting or changing rules in collaboration with other children in order to make the game more "fair" or more "fun." The types of board games that are usually played by children or families are also similar to games with rules because often the rules are adapted for younger children. For example, they might get extra turns or the goal of the game may not be to win but for all to finish together.

Play as a Venue for the Development of Social, Emotional, Moral, and Cognitive Abilities

In addition to Bruner, Piaget, and Vygotsky, there are many other theorists and researchers who have discussed the potential relationships among various types of play and child progress in specific developmental areas. In particular, the role of pretense in fostering social, emotional, language, and cognitive abilities has been discussed extensively and research studies examining various aspects of play that seem to be related to developmental growth have been proposed by numerous authors, although the evidence is mixed (Lillard et al. 2012).

Social Development through Play

Beginning in the mid-20th century (see Parten, 1933), observational studies of children's social development during play have been conducted. Parten's early studies described the typical social stages of play that can be observed in preschool children, which seemed to indicate developmental progress. For example, children typically progress from playing alone in parallel situations with other children and later engage in elaborated socially complex play scenarios. Smilansky (1968) conducted studies to observe whether growth in such skills could occur during sociodramatic play and found that both social pretense and language skills could be developed. Rubin and colleagues (Rubin, 1985; Coplan, Rubin, & Findlay, 2006) have reported that children who do not progress from solitary play to social play may have developmental difficulties at later ages, and authors have discussed how complex pretense scripts require children to understand roles and the behaviors required in various roles (e.g., Ariel, 2002; Vandenberg, 2004). Games with rules also have socio-moral components that must be addressed by children during their competitive game playing (DeVries, 2006).

Emotional Development through Play

The assertion that play has a role in supporting emotional health has a long history. Erikson (1977), Anna Freud (1928), and many others concerned with mental health issues of children have promoted the use of play therapy to assist children in gaining emotional control and healing. Also, therapists such as Greenspan (1990) have developed "floor-time" play techniques for parents and children with autistic spectrum disabilities. Although there are not as many studies specifically related to the role of play in assisting typically developing children's emotional development, Lillard et al. (2012) report that the studies that have been reported do indicate emotion regulation may be improved through pretend play. Vygotsky's view of elaborated pretense as a means of developing self-regulation skills has also been supported by research (see Bordrova & Leong, 2006).

Moral Development through Play

As noted earlier, Piaget (1965) described the role of games with rules as being involved in promoting children's moral development, especially in their moral reasoning. DeVries (2006), drawing on the work of Kohlberg (1987), has specifically investigated the moral dilemmas that arise when children play games together and has documented the issues that arise in such play. Recently Davis and Bergen (2014) have discussed the types and levels of moral development that college-age individuals report and compared those levels to the types of play that they reported at various age levels. They found that earlier pretend play, as well as games, appeared to be related to higher levels of moral development at college age.

Cognitive Development through Play

There are proponents of the view that cognitive development is highly related to play, especially to pretense, and there have been many studies that have reported relationships between play and various cognitive processes. For example, Russ (2013) makes the case for childhood pretense being the foundation for adult creativity, Roskos and Christie (2004) discuss how pretend play increases literacy development, Kamii et al. (2004) report how block building supports mathematical understanding, and Cooper and Robinson (1989) indicate the extent that certain types of childhood play is related to science and engineering careers.

The potential role of "embodied cognition," in which physical actions serve as a venue for thought, has been discussed by a number of theorists (see review by Wilson, 2002). From this theoretical perspective the workings of the human mind can be understood in the context of its interactive relationship to human bodily actions. This perspective suggests that the mind/body interactive connection is essential for human development because perceptual and motoric processing were the initiators of cognitive activity in evolutionary history. Whether such "embodied cognition" is an essential element for human development is being debated and it will be tested as technology-augmented play that does not require extensive bodily movement becomes more and more pervasive.

Brain Maturation, Play Development, and Other Developmental Areas as Nonlinear Dynamic Systems

Recently play development and brain maturation, as well as other developmental processes, have been characterized as nonlinear dynamic systems (Bergen, 2012; Fromberg, 2010; Vanderven, 2006). According to Guastello (1997), this perspective on human development is concerned with the analysis of the ways in which living systems show complex nonlinear dynamics that interact with other such systems and thus increase in complexity of interaction. Thelen and Smith (1994) have stated that nonlinear dynamic systems theory is the appropriate way to study human development processes because development is "modular, heterochronic, context-dependent, and multidimensional" (p. 121). Play development and brain maturation, as well as other developmental processes, exemplify many of the characteristics of nonlinear dynamic systems. They are complex phenomena that have not been well explained by linear systems thinking (van Geert, 2000).

Qualities of Nonlinear Dynamic Systems

Nonlinear dynamic systems theory, derived from fields such as biology, physics and mathematics, posits that changes over time among interrelated elements have complex and systematic interactions. The features of the theory that have relevance for human development systems have been outlined by Thelen and Smith (1994). They state that human development systems have multiple and continuous interactions at levels from molecular to cultural and these unfold over many time scales. Dynamic systems are multilayered and complex and their actions and interactions cannot be explained by linear, simple cause/effect research. Therefore, when studying the effects of particular phenomena (such as the effects of technology-augmented play materials on human development), the characteristics of the dynamic system must be considered. These are some of the characteristics of such systems that have been identified by Thelen (for further details, see Bergen, 2008, 2012). Such systems are:

> Self-organizing: *pattern and order emerge from interactions* of components of the complex system without having explicit instructions from the organism or the environment
> Nonlinear: development is *unidirectional* and proceeds in many interactive directions rather than in a linear fashion
> Open: the systems are organized by taking in *energy* from many sources
> Stable: there are *attractor* states in which the system establishes patterns of organization
> Changing: there are also states of change that show *soft assembly* and *sensitivity to initial conditions*
> Complex with *phase shifts*: periods of great change, drawn from many sources, may lead to major differences
> Novelty-prone: the organism shows great *flexibility*, especially to novel conditions

Brain Maturation as a Dynamic Systems Process

Brain research has provided evidence that brain development follows a nonlinear systems model (Bates, 2005). Even in the prenatal period, the brain shows *self-organization*, with patterns that spontaneously emerge from chaotic appearances. For example, during this period, the cortex is formed by neurons climbing "ladders" of glia cells to create the higher brain centers (Bergen & Coscia, 2001). *Sensitive dependence on initial conditions* is also evident, as research on the harmful effects of drugs or alcohol on the prenatal brain and abuse or neglect effects on infant brain development has shown (Perry, 1996; Carlson & Earls, 1997; Eliot, 1999). However, the brain also shows *openness*, receiving energy from outside sources as well as having *control parameters* that guide the developmental patterns of various parts of the brain. Some parameters are invariant (sensory locations), some change with age (frontal lobe development), and some change with experiences (synaptic connections). Behavioral evidence of *phase shifts* in brain development can be seen in the change in infant emotion and language once myelination begins to connect the limbic system with the frontal lobe. Although the brain is modular, with certain areas having some primary roles, it is also *interdependent*. *Soft assembly* is also a characteristic of the brain because it is flexible, with stable and dynamic qualities alternating; it is not "hard-wired." Thus, a primary characteristic of the brain is that of *plasticity*, because the capacity for brain system change is always present. There are periods of both *attractor* states and periods of *disequilibrium*. *Recursion* is also present in the brain because brain development is repetitive, with elaborations both across brain areas and across developmental age in self-similar patterns. The *fractal* quality can be seen in the repeating patterns of development as each area of the brain becomes activated, and in the nested quality of many brain functions.

Play Development as a Dynamic Systems Process

Play development also meets dynamic systems criteria. Play is a *self-organizing* system that may appear chaotic but that moves toward order, involving spontaneously emerging patterns of *attractor* states. Play involves *phase shifts*, which are abrupt changes in play patterns that lead to higher levels of play, but the play state also shows *disequilibrium*, because it is always capable of change. Play usually has *recursive* elements with elaborations and self-similar patterns within each developmental age. These systems of repeated patterns are often labeled "practice play." Play also exemplifies the characteristic of *sensitive dependence on initial conditions* because small inputs into play situations may cause disparate results. The types of materials, the time available for play, the settings in which it can occur, and the materials available all influence the character of pretense. Play demonstrates *openness* because the players continue to receive energy from sources outside the "playframe" (Bateson, 1956). It also involves *control parameters*, such as differences in play patterns due to age and skill of players, limitations on experience, types of settings available for play, and player-defined rules in games. Play shows *interdependence* because all levels of play are interrelated and because of its *soft assembly*, play has both stable and dynamic alternating periods and thus is not "hard-wired." Play epitomizes *plasticity* because capacity for change is always present. Thus, play also can be characterized as a nonlinear dynamic system.

Dynamic Interactions of Brain Maturation and Typical Play Development

There are many ways that typical playful behavior at various ages reflects maturation of certain brain areas. For example, during the infant period, as the sensorimotor areas of the brain develop, infants enjoy looking and reaching for objects, hearing and making interesting sounds, and engaging in exploratory play. When sensory and motor areas gain greater synaptic connections, practice play involving repeating and elaborating on actions becomes the most common play type. Piaget saw this practice play as evidence of "thought in action" and Bruner would agree that this shows "enactive" thought. As the emotional brain centers begin to connect to frontal lobe brain areas, social-emotional play, such as peek-a-boo and other turn-taking games begin. At the end of the first year, when the higher brain centers where language and conceptual thought are primarily located begin to mature, play with language and pretend play begin.

Toddler play reflects the continuing development of the frontal cortex, the site of symbolic thought, through their initiation of such pretense, which becomes a major play mode by age 3. Studies of the concept "theory of mind" (ability to imagine what others are thinking) have indicated that toddlers demonstrate that first in pretense and older toddlers are able to implement simple scripts with two or three action elements. Although practice play remains a major mode, it often has elements of construction and pretense. For example, a "garage" for a car might be made with a few blocks. Another element of brain maturation is shown in toddler language play and expressions of humor, which result from observing or performing incongruous events, such as putting a hat on a dog figure.

By early childhood, sociodramatic pretense involving elaborate scripts and set designs appear and games with rules become more complex. Construction involves designing settings for play as well as creating art and designs. There is a great deal of discussion of "fair" rules in games and there are many symbolic games that children play. Practice play continues to be prominent, with bike riding, skating, and other tests of skill of prime interest. These more elaborate manifestations of play give evidence of the synaptogenic and pruning processes occurring during this age period. During middle childhood the extensive and elaborative private pretense, which may involve sets and scripts that continue for many weeks, also gives evidence to the refining of brain structures and functions. Practice play, however, may be more in the service of sports at this age, for example, repeatedly shooting baskets into the net on the garage wall. Many elements of play first seen in middle childhood are continued in adolescence, such as risk-taking physical activities such as rope climbing and playing elaborate symbolic games. Although sports may take the place of most play for some adolescents, many adolescents engage in fantasy pretense (daydreaming, writing poetry, composing music) and enjoy performing in actual plays or having hobbies such as collecting sports figures. Many of the risk-taking types of playful activities in which adolescents engage give evidence that limbic and frontal lobe maturation is not yet completed.

Whether and how the presence of technology-augmented play materials may differentially affect these dynamic interactions of brain maturation and play development are unclear, however. Before evaluating the potential ways technology-augmented toys can affect various areas of human development, it is important to consider the many meanings the term "technology" has embraced.

Defining Technology

The definitions of the meanings and connotations of technology range from simple to complex. For example, the *Encyclopedia Britannica* provides a broad but accessible definition of technology, as "the application of scientific knowledge to the practical aims of human life or, as it is sometimes phrased, to the change and manipulation of the human environment" (www.britannica.com). There are other perspectives that capture the scope and variability of the concept, however. For example, Heidegger (1977) argued that technology is a way of thinking that reveals an essence of efficiency for its own sake. According to Heidegger, technology should not be defined just by its instrumental purposes because then "we remain held fast in the will to master it" (p. 32). We should have a broader definition and move beyond values such as efficiency. Batteau (2009, 2010) delineated between "tools" and "technology," and argued that technology embraces increasing complexity, autonomy, and connectedness. He embedded technology firmly within "sociotechnical networks" (Batteau, 2009, p. 11) and suggested that technology could not exist outside the frame of the networks because of its effect on culture and culture's effect on technology.

Another theorist, Arthur (2009) defined technology in three ways: 1) "a means to fulfill a human purpose," 2) "an assemblage of practices and components," and 3) "a collection of devices and engineering practices available to a culture" (p. 28). For Arthur, this definition was critical because he asserted that how humans think of technology will determine how they think of its creation. Feenberg (2006), however, argued for a definition of technology that spans two dimensions, namely values and agency. Technology can be seen as either value-neutral or value-laden and either autonomous or humanly controlled. Feenberg suggests that humans will "inevitably address the question of technology along with many other questions that hang in suspense today" (p. 15). However, Poster (2001) asserts that "the term *technology* is particularly misleading in the age of 'smart machines'" (p. 21). The only modifier for *technology*, "high technology," refers to advanced assemblages of machines but it "does not distinguish clearly between particular types such as mechanical or electrical" (p. 21). Although the definitions of technology are complex, the definition used in this book is closer to the generally accepted and accessible definitions. That is, the authors suggest that technology-augmented play materials apply "scientific knowledge" to human play experiences and involve the "change and manipulation of the human environment."

Technological Invention as a Dynamic Systems Process

Human technological invention and discovery also have the characteristic qualities of nonlinear dynamic systems. For example, although inventors initially have some type of plan in mind, much of technological change results from *self-organizing* aspects inherent in the technological systems, which have *chaotic* as well as ordered qualities. There are periods of systematic discovery in which inventions have emerging patterns of *attractor* states that dominate. However, there are also *phase shifts*, in which abrupt changes in technological thought lead to extensions and differentiations in technological creations. Therefore, technology development also shows *disequilibrium*, because it is always capable of change. New technological inventions usually have *recursive* elements that involve elaborations of similar patterns drawn from earlier ideas. Technology invention also exemplifies the characteristic of *sensitive dependence on initial conditions* because small inputs into a technological process may cause disparate new materials or products. The types of materials, the time and support for technological invention, the settings in which it can occur, and the materials available all influence the character of technological creativity and invention. These also demonstrate *openness* because those involved in technology invention receive energy from many sources outside the existing frames of understanding and *soft assembly*, because technological creativity has both stable and dynamic alternating periods. Technological invention epitomizes system *plasticity* because the capacity for change is always present. Of course, there are also *control parameters* that depend on differences in past technological knowledge, the creativity and skill of inventors, limitations in their experience, the types of settings available for invention, and the *openness* of the cultural system to new technological ideas. Thus, technological invention demonstrates *interdependence* because there are many levels of interaction.

Dynamic Interactions of Brain Maturation, Play Development, and Technology-Augmented Play

The dynamic interactions of technology-augmented toys and devices—such as "talking" toys, video games, and phone apps—with brain development and with play development are likely to affect the domain-general capacity of the neurally plastic brain, resulting in "pluripotentiality" (Bates, 2005) of possibilities. Cortical structures can be configured in many ways, depending on types and timing of experiences, which enable the brain to adapt to a variety of different "brain plans." Research on the nature of play has shown that it also exemplifies pluripotentiality, continually adapting to environmental conditions and developmental changes (Vanderven, 2006). Because the play environment for children and adolescents has changed greatly with the advent of technology-augmented play materials, all of the dynamic system factors that have affected brain and play interactions with traditional play materials are now also being affected by technology-augmented play materials. Since brain maturation is influenced by whatever experiences the individual encounters, it is likely that changes in child and adolescent play experiences will differentially interact with brain maturation factors, resulting in "future brains" that differ from those humans have today. These factors will also affect the development of social, emotional, moral, and cognitive abilities, which will exhibit pluripotentiality in future generations.

FIGURE 1.1 These animals are going to the farm.

FIGURE 1.2 I'm talking to mommy.

FIGURE 1.3 Can the dolls go into the doll house?

Activities and Questions for Discussion

1. Think back to your childhood years. What were the play activities that were of most interest to you and how do you think they affected your brain maturation and subsequent behaviors?

FIGURE 1.4 This is my favorite hat!

2. Talk to your parents or other people in your family about their remembrances of their play experiences. What ways are they different from those of yours and your friends? How do you think they may have affected their brain maturation and subsequent behaviors?
3. Read the book, *The Velveteen Rabbit* (Williams-Bianco, 1926). Write a paragraph about what you think the author was trying to express about the developmental meaning of such traditional, non-technology-augmented toys. Speculate about how technology-augmented toys could or could not have the same developmental meaning.

References

Ariel, S. (2002). *Children's imaginative play: A visit to wonderland.* Westport, CN: Praeger.

Arthur, W.B. (2009). *The nature of technology: What it is and how it evolves.* New York: Simon and Schuster.

Baird, A.A., Gruber, S.A., Fein, D.A., Maas, L.C., Steingard, R.J., & Renshaw, J.F. (1999). Functional magnetic resonance imaging of facial affect recognition in children and adolescents. *Journal of the American Academy of Child and Adolescent Psychiatry, 2,* 195–199.

Bates, E. (2005). Plasticity, localization, and language development. In S.T. Parker, J. Langer, C. Milbrath (Eds.), *Biology and knowledge revisited: From neurogenesis to psychogenesis* (pp. 205–254). New York: Psychology Press.

Bateson, G. (1956). The message "This is play." In B. Schaffner (Ed.), *Group processes: Transactions of the second conference* (pp. 145–241). New York: Josiah Macy, Jr. Foundation.

Batteau, A.W. (2009). *Technology and culture.* Long Grove, IL: Waveland Press.

Batteau, A.W. (2010). Technological peripheralization. *Science, Technology, and Human Values, 35*(4), 554–574.

Bauer, P.J., Lukowski, A.F., & Pathman, T. (2010). Neuropsychology of middle childhood development (6 to 11 years old). In A. Davis (Ed.), *Handbook of pediatric neuropsychology* (pp. 37–46). New York: Springer.

Bergen, D. (2008). *Human development: Traditional and contemporary theories.* Upper Saddle River, NJ: Pearson/Prentice-Hall.

Bergen, D. (2009). Play as the learning medium for future scientists, mathematicians, and engineers. *American Journal of Play, 1*(4), 1–10.

Bergen, D. (2012). Play, technology toy affordances, and brain development: Considering research and policy issues. In S. Waite-Stupiansky & L. Cohen (Eds.), *Play: A polyphony of research, theories and issues (Volume 12)* (pp. 163–174). Lanham, MD: Information Age.

Bergen, D., & Coscia, J.M. (2001). *Brain research and childhood education: Implications for educators.* Olney, MD: Association for Childhood Education International. [Translated and published in China, 2006]

Bergen, D., & Woodin, M. (2010). Neuropsychological development of newborns, infants, and toddlers (0–3). In A. Davis (Ed.), *Handbook of pediatric neuropsychology* (pp. 13–30). New York: Springer.

Bordrova, E., & Leong, D.J. (2006). Adult influences on play: The Vygotskian approach. In D.P. Fromberg & D. Bergen (Eds.), *Play from birth to twelve: Contexts, perspectives, and meanings* (2nd ed., pp. 167–172). New York: Routledge.

Bronk, K. C. (2010). Neuropsychology of adolescent development (12 to 18 years). In A. Davis, (Ed.), *Handbook of pediatric neuropsychology* (pp. 45–57). New York: Springer.

Bruner, J.S. (1964). The course of cognitive growth. *American Psychologist, 19*(1), 1–15.

Carlson, M., & Earls, F. (1997). Psychological and neuroendocrinolgical sequelae of early social deprivation in institutionalized children in Romania. In C.S. Carter, I.I. Lederhendler, & B. Kirkpatrick (Eds.), *The integrative neurobiology of affiliation* (pp. 419–428). New York: New York Academy of Sciences.

Comenius, J.A. (1632/1907). *Didactic magna.* London: A. C. Black.

Comenius, J.A. (1657/1967). *Orbis pictus.* London: Oxford University Press.

Cooper, S., & Robinson, D.A. (1989). The influence of gender and anxiety on mathematics performance. *Journal of College Student Development, 30*(5), 459–461.

Coplan, R.J., Rubin, K.H., & Findlay, L.C. (2006). Social and nonsocial play. In D.P. Fromberg & D. Bergen (Eds.), *Play from birth to twelve: Contexts, perspectives, and meanings* (2nd ed., pp. 87–102). New York: Routledge.

Darwin, C. (1859). *The origin of species.* Reprint. New York: Modern Library.

Davis, D., & Bergen, D. (2014). Relationships among play behaviors reported by college students and their responses to moral issues: A pilot study. *Journal of Research in Childhood Education, 28*, 484–498.

DeVries, R. (2006). Games with rules. In D.P. Fromberg & D. Bergen (Eds.), *Play from birth to twelve: Contexts, perspectives, and meanings* (2nd ed., pp. 119–126). New York: Routledge.

Dewey, J. (1910/1997). *How we think.* Toronto: Dover.

Dewey, J. (1916). *Democracy and education.* New York: Macmillan.

Eliot, L. (1999). *What's going on in there: How the brain and mind develop in the first five years of life.* New York: Bantam.

Ellis, M.J. (1998). Play and the origin of the species. In D. Bergen (Ed.) *Readings from Play as a learning medium* (pp. 29–31). Olney, MD: ACEI.

Erikson, E.H. (1977). *Toys and reason.* New York: Norton.

Fagen, R. (1981). *Animal play behavior.* Oxford: Oxford University Press.

Feenberg, A. (2006). What is philosophy of technology? In J.R. Dakers (Ed.), *Defining technological literacy: Towards an epistemological framework* (pp. 5–16). New York: Palgrave Macmillan.

Forman, G. (2006). Constructive play. In D.P. Fromberg & D. Bergen (Eds.), *Play from birth to twelve: Contexts, perspectives, and meanings* (2nd ed., pp. 103–110). New York: Routledge.

Freud, A. (1928). *Introduction to the techniques of child analysis.* New York: Nervous and Mental Disease Publishing.

Freysinger, V. (2006). Play in the context of life-span human development. In D.P. Fromberg & D. Bergen (Eds.), *Play from birth to twelve: Contexts, perspectives, and meanings* (2nd ed., pp. 53–62). New York: Routledge.

Froebel, F. (1887). *The education of man.* New York: Appleton-Century.

Fromberg, D.P. (2010). How nonlinear systems inform meaning and early education. *Nonlinear Dynamics, Psychology, and Life Sciences, 14*(1), 47–68.

Giedd, J.N., & Rapoport, J.L. (2010). Structural MRI of pediatric brain development: What have we learned and where are we going? *Neuron, 67*(5), 728–734.

Greenspan, S.I. (1990). How emotional development relates to learning. In S. Hanna & S. Wilford (Eds.), *Floor time: Tuning in to each child* (pp. 1–4). New York: Scholastic.

Guastello, S.J. (1997). Science evolves: An introduction to nonlinear dynamics, psychology, and life sciences. *Nonlinear Dynamics, Psychology, and Life Sciences, 1*(1), 1–6.

Haier, J. (1993). Cerebral glucose metabolism and intelligence. In P.A. Vernon (Ed.), *Biological approaches to the study of human intelligence* (pp. 317–332). Norwood, NJ: Ablex.

Hall, G.S. (1920). *Youth.* New York: Appleton-Century.

Hall, G.S. (1924). *Adolescence: Its psychology and its relations to physiology, anthropology, sociology, sex, crime, religion and education.* New York: D. Appleton.

Heidegger, M. (1977). *The question of technology and other essays.* Trans. W. Lovett. New York: Harper and Row.

Huizinga, J. (1950). *Homo Ludens: A study of the play-element in culture.* London: Routledge & Kegan Paul.

Hutt, C. (1971). Exploration and play in children. In R.E. Herron & B. Sutton-Smith (Eds.), *Child's play* (pp. 231–252). New York: Wiley.

Iwaniuk, A.N., Nelson, J.E., & Pellis, S.M. (2001). Do big-brained animals play more? Comparative analysis of play and relative brain size in mammals. *Journal of Comparative Psychology, 115*(1), 29–41.

Kamii, C., Miyakawa, Y., & Kato, Y. (2004). The development of logico-mathematical knowledge in a block building activity at ages 1–4. *Journal of Research in Childhood Education, 19*(1), 44–57.

Kitayama, S. (2013). Mapping mindsets: The world of cultural neuroscience. *Observer, 26*(10), 21–23.

Kohlberg, L. (1987). *Child psychology and childhood education: A cognitive-developmental view.* New York: Longman.

Lezak, M.D., Howieson, D.B., & Loring, D.W. (2004). *Neuropsychological assessment* (4th ed.). New York: Oxford.

Lillard, A.S., Lerner, M.D., Hopkins, E.J., Dore, R.A., Smith, E.D., & Palmquist, C.M. (2012). The impact of pretend play on children's development: A review of the evidence. *Psychological Bulletin.* Advance online publication.

Lorenz, K. (1971). *Studies in animal and human behavior.* New York: Methuen.

Morris, S. R. (1998). No learning by coercion: Paidia and Paideia in Platonic philosophy. In D. P. Fromberg & D. Bergen (Eds.), *Play from birth to twelve and beyond: Contexts, perspectives, and meanings* (pp. 109–118). New York: Garland.

Opie, I., & Opie, P. (1969). *Children's play in streets and playgrounds*. London: Clarendon Press.

Parten, M. (1933). Social play among preschool children. *Journal of Abnormal and Social Psychology, 28*, 136–147.

Pellis, S.M., & Iwaniuk, A.N. (2004). Evolving a playful brain: A levels of control approach. *International Journal of Comparative Psychology, 17*, 92–118.

Perry, B. (1996). Incubated in terror: Neurodevelopmental factors in the "cycle of violence." In J.D. Osofsky (Ed.), *Children, youth, and violence: Searching for solutions* (pp. 2–20), New York: Guildford.

Piaget, J. (1945). *Play, dreams and imitation in childhood*. London: Heinemann.

Piaget, J. (1965). *The moral judgment of the child*. New York: Norton.

Plato. (360 BC). *Laws*, (1942) translator R. G. Bury London: Heinemann.

Poster, M. (2001). *What's the matter with the internet? (Vol. 3)*. University of Minnesota Press.

Rizzolatti, G., & Craighero, L. (2004). The mirror-neuron system. *Annual Review of Neuroscience, 27*, 169–192.

Root-Bernstein, M.M., & Root-Bernstein, R.S. (2006). Imaginary worldplay in childhood and maturity and its impact on adult creativity. *Creativity Research Journal, 18*, 402–425.

Roskos, K., & Christie, J. (2004). Examining the play-literacy interface: A critical review and future directions. In E. Zigler, D. Singer, & S. Bishop-Josef (Eds.), *Children's play: The roots of reading* (pp. 95–123). Washington, DC: Zero to Three Press.

Rousseau, J.J. (1792/1911). *Emile*. New York: E.P. Dutton.

Rubin, K.H. (1985). Nonsocial play in preschoolers: Necessary evil? *Child Development, 53*, 651–657.

Russ, S.W. (2013). *Pretend play in childhood: Foundation of adult creativity*. Washington, DC: American Psychological Association.

Shore, R. (1997). *Rethinking the brain: New insights into early development*. New York: Families and Work Institute.

Smilansky, S. (1968). *The effects of sociodramatic play on disadvantaged preschool children*. New York: Wiley.

Sowell, E.R., Thompson, P. M., Holmes, C.J., Jernigan, T.L., & Toga, A.W. (1999). In vivo evidence for post-adolescent brain maturation in frontal and striatal regions. *Nature Neuroscience, 2*(10), 859–861.

Technology (n.d.). In *Encyclopedia Britannica*. Available at: www.britannica.com

Thelen, E., & Smith, L.B. (1994). *A dynamic systems approach to the development of cognition and action*. Boston: MIT Press.

Vandenberg, B. (2004). Real and not real: A vital developmental dichotomy. In E. Zigler, D. Singer, & S. Bishop-Josef (Eds.), *Children's play; The roots of reading* (pp. 49–58). Washington, DC: Zero to Three Press.

Vanderven, K. (2006). Play, proteus, and paradox: Education for a chaotic and supersymmetric world. In D.P. Fromberg & D. Bergen (Eds.), *Play from birth to twelve and beyond: Contexts, perspectives, and meanings* (2nd ed., pp. 405–516). New York: Garland.

van Geert, P. (2000). The dynamics of general developmental mechanisms: From Piaget and Vygotsky to dynamic systems models. *Current Directions in Psychological Science, 9*, 64–88.

Vygotsky, L.S. (1962). *Thought and language*. Cambridge, MA: MIT Press.

Vygotsky, L.S. (1967). Play and its role in the mental development of the child. *Soviet Psychology, 5*, 6–18.

Washburn, S.L., & Howell, F.C. (1960). Human evolution and culture. In S. Tax & C. Callendar (Eds.), *The evolution of man (Vol. 2)*. Chicago: University of Chicago Press.

Whiting, B., & Pope Edwards, C. (1988). *Children of different worlds: The formation of social behavior*. Cambridge, MA: Harvard University Press.

Williams-Bianco, M. (1926). *The velveteen rabbit: or, How toys become real*. Pioneer Drama Service, Inc.

Wilson, M. (2002). Six views of embodied cognition. *Psychonomic Bulletin & Review, 9*(4), 625–636.

2

CHANGES IN PLAY ENVIRONMENTS WITH ADVENT OF TECHNOLOGY-AUGMENTED PLAY MATERIALS

Representation Modes and Affordances within Physical and Virtual Contexts

---

The Streeters had their first baby a year ago but they live over 200 miles from Joe Streeter's parents. His parents visited at the time of the baby's birth but they did not visit again until the baby, Jonah, was about 4 or 5 months old. When they observed the diaper-changing routine on the second visit, they were completely amazed at how efficiently that process was accomplished because Joe gave Jonah his iPhone™ to hold while he changed the diaper. Jonah spent the tIme quietly observing the animated designs on the phone and was completely absorbed in the phone rather than in his parent's actions. Joe's parents remembered spending time talking, singing, and playing baby games to hold Joe's interest when they did diaper changing and they wondered what is gained and what is lost when technology-augmented devices become the focus of the baby's attention rather than the parent during such routine daily activities that are involved in raising children.

Over the course of history, humans have made many technological changes to their environment to fulfill various human purposes or improve practical aims and solve problems. Older examples of such technology inventions that are still used today include tools such as forks, combs, shovels, hammers, and drums. Some of the earlier technology that resulted in major environmental manipulations and societal changes include transportation inventions (the wheeled cart, boats, trains, automobiles, and planes), clothing manufacturing methods (needles for sewing, looms, sewing machines), and communication tools (paper and writing tools, typewriters, telegraph machines). Early play materials for children such as dolls, rocking horses, and puzzles are also examples of ways that humans have changed and manipulated play environments through the design of objects that may or may not exist in the natural world. Thus, technological innovation has always been a part of human experience and most of these creations have altered human behavior (and possibly human brain maturation!) in various ways. Some of these technologies have enhanced specific aspects of human life (e.g., water purification systems) and some have had negative as well as positive consequences (e.g., hydraulic fracturing, genetically altered seeds). Because technology creates changing environments to meet human identified needs, it is a multidimensional concept, involving values and social consequences, and engendering various perspectives, some of which stress positive and life enhancing aspects and some that result in more problematic consequences. Often the same technology innovation may result in both positive and negative consequences for human life, and many of these consequences may be unforeseen when they are first initiated.

The technological innovations in present day society are affecting many aspects of modern life, including the play environments of infants, children, and adolescents. There are basic differences between the play environments of children growing up in earlier times and the present-day play environment. For example, children from previous generations had access to a greater range of "natural" play materials (rocks, sticks, streams) and to a much smaller range of deliberately designed play materials. Also, earlier play materials had few "active" qualities that enabled the toy to initiate child responses. Dolls may have made a crying sound when hugged, toy cars may have accelerated faster when pushed, and blocks shapes and sizes may have affected the types of buildings that could be constructed. However, for toys of the past, the most engaging qualities of the toys came from human action. That is, children's voices made the doll "talk," their active running made the plane "fly," and their creative ideas made the small-world "story plots" that the toys enacted. These changes in play settings, materials, and experiences are likely to affect other aspects of human development, including human brain maturation. There is research evidence that adults of today remember somewhat different play experiences than adults of earlier times recall.

Research Studies on Adult Memories of Childhood Play

The authors have conducted a number of studies of what adults reported as their most salient childhood play and their views of its value. The first compared the memories of play of American and Chinese young adults (Bergen, Liu, & Liu, 1997). The second surveyed different groups of young adults at three different time periods and compared their remembrances of play and opinions of its value (Bergen, 2003; Bergen & Williams, 2008). Recently two more studies of the types of play at four age levels reported by college-age students have been conducted (Davis & Bergen, 2014; 2015).

The study that compared the memories of Chinese and American students found that both groups were comparable in regard to describing their remembered play as being primarily pretense and games with rules, and both groups described much of their play as being outdoors. The specific games and pretense themes differed, however. The second study, which compared results of the American student sample from the first study with results of two studies of later cohorts of students using the same procedures, found significant differences on a number of dimensions. There were 201 students in the 1990 study, 137 in the 2000 study, and 209 in the 2008 study. In all three groups pretense was the most reported type of play during the elementary age period, most of it occurring in private spaces (basements, yards) or with small-scale objects (dolls, action figures). Games with rules (ball games, traditional games) were the second most reported type of play at all time periods. Also, all groups reported they played outdoors but the earlier groups reported that their play ranged throughout their neighborhood and involved other children while the latter group reported more play in their own yard and playing alone about 25% of the time. The first group reported no play with technology-augmented play materials but the other two groups reported about 7–9% of their play being with such materials. At all three periods the major reason reported for play was "fun" and the two major types of learning from the play mentioned were "social skills" and "imagination/creativity."

In the study Davis and Bergen conducted more recently, the college students described their play at four age levels: preschool age, elementary age, high school age, and college age. They reported that at preschool age the play included pretense with dolls and action figures, games such as hide and seek, practice play such as swimming or riding bikes, and technology play such as videogames and TV watching. At elementary age, their play continued to include pretense as well as games, including board games. Their reported practice play was similar to preschool age; however, construction with small blocks (e.g., Legos™) and building forts and other structures also were mentioned often. Technology play included video gaming with friends and computer game play. By adolescence, they did not report pretend play but they were involved in pretense-related activities such as being in plays and dancing, as well as involved in games such as bowling, biking and other active practice play. The types of technology play they reported included video games and play with online computer games. Figures 2.1–2.4 show percent of time reported for play activities at the various ages. Note that the percentage of reported technology-augmented play is greater at later age levels but that there is still a balance of reported play-related activities at later ages. All of these young people grew up, of course, before the advent of smart phones, tablets, apps, and other technology-augmented devices to which today's children are exposed.

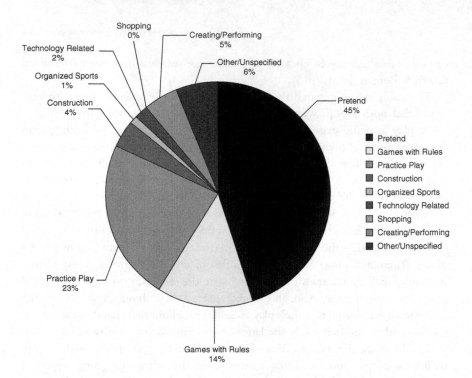

FIGURE 2.1 College–Age Adults' Memories of Childhood Play: Childhood Age

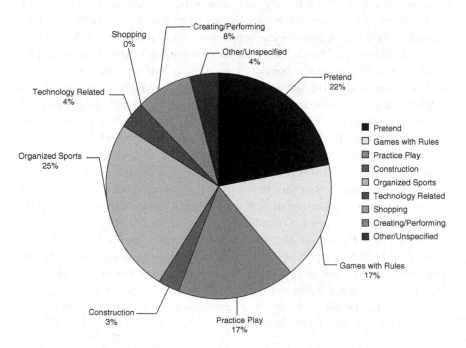

FIGURE 2.2 College–Age Adults' Memories of Childhood Play: Elementary Age

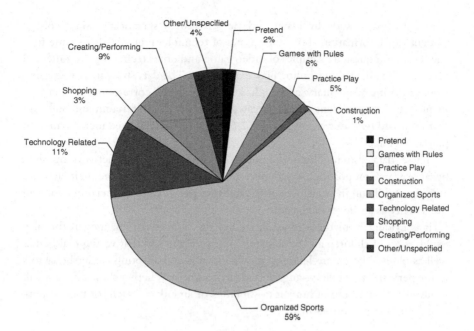

FIGURE 2.3 College-Age Adults' Memories of Childhood Play: High School Age

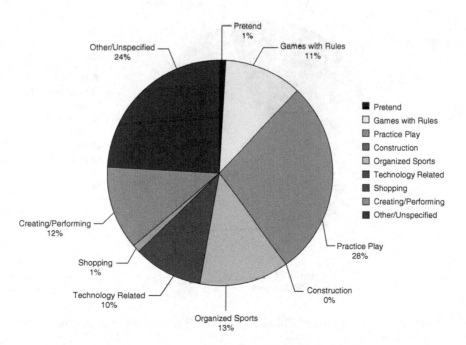

FIGURE 2.4 College-Age Adults' Memories of Childhood Play: College Age

A subsequent study by Davis and Bergen (2015) specifically asked college students for information about their types of technology play at these same four age levels. It requested examples of video game and other technology-augmented play and also asked about online play experiences. The data show increased game playing during elementary and high school ages, and corresponding increases in play involving violent games as categorized by the Entertainment Software Rating Board (www.esrb.org). Figures 2.5–2.8 show the reported increase in such play at later ages.

These data also highlight the rapid expansion of social networking sites, because a large proportion of students reported that these sites were their favorites at high school and in college. Figure 2.9 shows the increase in social networking site activity as age level increased.

It is evident from these research studies that long-term changes in the play experiences of children and adolescents are occurring and that young children as well as older children are learning new behaviors and adapting earlier behaviors to the pervasive technology-augmented environment. Whether these changes will result in a diminishing of human possibilities or an enhancement of human possibilities is an open question.

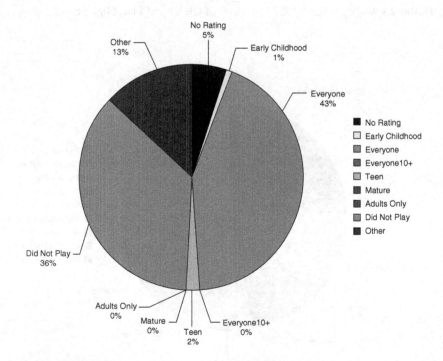

FIGURE 2.5 ESRB Rating of College-Age Adults Reported Technology-Augmented Play: Preschool Age

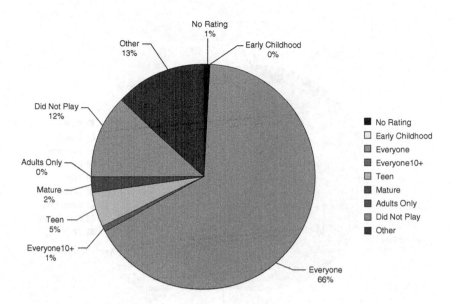

FIGURE 2.6 ESRB Rating of College-Age Adults Reported Technology-Augmented Play: Elementary Age

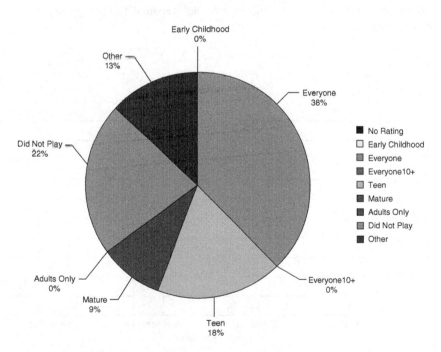

FIGURE 2.7 ESRB Rating of College-Age Adults Reported Technology-Augmented Play: Adolescent Age

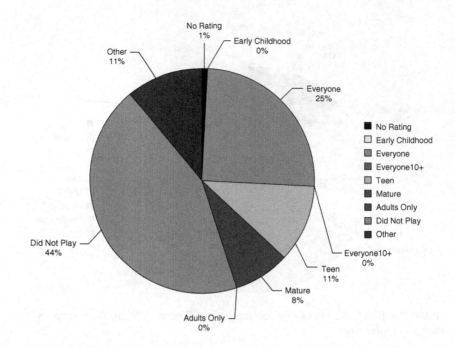

FIGURE 2.8 ESRB Rating of College-Age Adults Reported Technology-Augmented Play: College Age

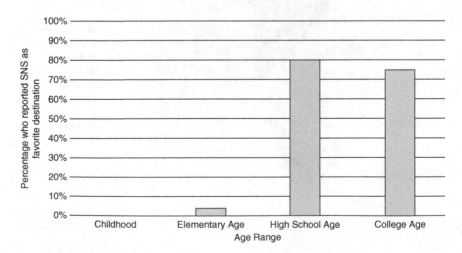

FIGURE 2.9 Social Network Services Reported Preference Across the Ages

Views on Potential Effects of Technology-Augmented Play

Although the body of research on effects of technology-augmented play is still relatively small (Wartella, Caplovitz, & Lee, 2004), a number of authors have expressed their views on the potential positive and negative effects of these changes in play materials. Their analyses are often widely different. Goldstein (2013) has stated that these devices have changed the play landscape because the players can not only play with the media but can change the shape of the games and, thus, this play also changes the players. He asserts that since toys have always been the means by which children learn about the values and practices of their culture, the technology-augmented environment is providing that cultural information today. In a discussion of effects of the pervasive technology-augmented culture, however, Levin (2013) argues that many of the cultural messages children receive are gender stereotypic or violent. She suggests that firsthand experiences communicated by families, teachers, and the community remain important.

Kafai (2006) has discussed how the feedback and feelings of control provided by video games can be valuable. She considers technology-augmented play materials as the new "playground" for today's children and recommends that children play with programmable building blocks, computational game tool kits, and virtual playgrounds, which all provide constructive activity because these types of technology-augmented play can provide the same values as blocks, Tinker Toys, Legos, and other concrete building materials. She does concede, however, that many present interactive technology play materials "undervalue the constructive aspects of play in which children have always engaged" (p. 213).

Lim and Clark (2010) assert that virtual worlds provide almost all of the advantages that typical play provides. Many of today's toys have an "online presence" allowing children to expand their world out of their "safe" home environment, thus taking the place of the wide-ranging neighborhood play of children in the past. Also, they state that online play with avatars expands the possibilities of imaginative play and supports "cultural convergence" and learning experiences. Jenkins (2009) suggests that the new skills learned through such play are ones needed in the future. For example, distributed cognition, identity performance, simulation, and navigation in multiple modalities are needed skills promoted by technology-augmented media. However, other writers state that the effects of highly specialized toys are currently unknown, and some research supports the view that these toys offer more negatives than positives. For example, after researching 3–6-year-olds' play with the robotic toy AIBO™, Kahn and colleagues (2004) concluded that the play resulted in "impoverished" relationships.

Views of the effects of technology-augmented play materials often vary depending on the age-level of the children who are the focus of the technology. Thus, a recent product designed for infants that would permit an electronic tablet to be positioned on their "bouncy chairs" or "potty chairs" was highly critiqued by advocacy groups that are opposing such "electronic babysitter" apps being promoted as ways to help brain development by manufacturers of these devices (Kang, 2013). In fact, the American Academy of Pediatrics has stated that infants under age 2 should have no "screen time," including time on mobile devices (2001, 2013). Similarly, adolescents' pervasive use of apps on various devices has been questioned in a recent work by Gardner and Davis (2013) because these virtual connections give adolescents the feeling that they are having close connections but really their connections are shallow rather than deep and sustained.

The use of electronic tablets as learning devices for preschool and elementary age children and children with special needs also have been interpreted both positively and negatively. For example, one study reported that digital media use enhanced attention, concentration levels, and knowledge levels of young children (Plowman, Stevenson, Stephan, & McPake, 2012) while a review of studies measuring learning effects of such use with children with special needs concluded that most effects are small or mixed, although "engagement" is increased (Weigel, Martin, & Bennett, 2010). On the other hand, when a robotics program designed for improving literacy skills of low-income high school students was studied, results showed improvement in science literacy skills for one of the cultural groups and improvement in mathematics and literacy skills for another cultural group. The authors concluded that low-income students might find robotics instruction helpful (Erdogan, Corlu, & Capraro, 2013).

Although such changes in play experiences will be especially influential on brain development during the infant and preschool age periods due to the extensive "brain building" that goes on during those years, because brain maturation continues to occur throughout childhood and into the adolescent and young adult years, the types of play that are pervasive during the entire period of brain development will have lasting effects on the physical, cognitive, social, and emotional development of the human species. Thus, it is important to have criteria for evaluating how the changing landscape of the play environment may affect long-term brain development and subsequent human evolution.

The authors have identified three ways to evaluate and understand the changing landscape of the play environment, which include examining the *representation modes* elicited, the *affordances* provided by the play materials, and the *context*s within which they exist. These criteria may enhance human ability to judge the play-supporting features of technology-augmented play materials, to compare such features to those of typical play materials, and to speculate about their potential effects on the long-term development of children and adolescents, as well as on the human species as a whole. These criteria can be used to judge the play supporting features of technology-augmented materials and their potential effects on the development of play skills, brain development, and social engagement of children and adolescents.

Criteria for Evaluating Technology-Augmented Play Materials: Representation Modes, Affordances, and Contexts

Although there would be many ways to evaluate the influence of technology-augmented play materials, there are some constructs that seem to be especially suited to be used to consider effects on brain maturation, as well as on social, emotional, moral, and cognitive development. These include examining the representation modes, the affordances, and contexts related to technology-augmented play.

Representation Modes

Bruner's (1964) designation of the three representation modes that may affect levels of cognitive understanding can be used to evaluate the effects of play materials. *Enactive* representation (interactive motoric responses) of knowledge varies greatly with differences in play materials. For example, children use their whole bodies during play with balls or climbing equipment while they primarily use eyes, hands, and fingers when playing a video game. In many traditional types of play there is also involvement of the mirror neurons because interpretation of the actions of other players is needed for social play. These whole body and face-to-face human interactions appear to be essentially present for young children's learning in many spheres, although such opportunities are more limited in many types of technology-augmented play. *Iconic* representations, on the other hand, are pervasively evident in many technology-augmented play materials. That is, the images on the computer screen "stand for" the actual objects and thus they are substituted for enactive experiences. For example, on the electronic tablet the pictures that stand for the "blocks" are stacked and the "bird" flies into a virtual sky.

The highest level of cognitive representation, the *symbolic*, which involves interpreting arbitrary code of language or other symbols, is also incorporated in many technology-augmented play materials, although this dimension varies with the complexity of such materials. For young children, there may be number or letter symbols that can be activated in various ways to "stand for" pictures of a number of objects or familiar animals. Young humans typically have engaged in all three of these representation modes during their developmental progress, so if there is a change in the balance of these modes of cognition during childhood, there may be some effects on social, emotional, moral, and cognitive development. Thus, one method of evaluating the potential effects of technology-augmented play is to examine whether the play materials involve one or more of these representation modes, and thus, potentially activate varied levels of social, emotion, moral, and cognitive engagement.

Affordances

According to Eleanor Gibson, who studied how humans directly perceive objects, every object in the environment provides affordances that elicit actions. That is, they suggest the ways in which the object can be perceived and acted upon by the perceiver (Gibson, 1969). The affordances of objects and other environmental features can be directly perceived by individuals without the need for cognitive interpretations, and they can have a great effect on the actions of the perceivers. Affordances of materials may be general or they may be specific; that is, they may suggest many actions that the perceiver can do with the object or they may dictate a narrow range of actions. Thus, the affordances of an object may promote either routinized or creative interactions. Lauren Resnick (1994) has explained that cognition is "situated" and that young children construct cognitive schema (organizing designs that impose structure on the environment) when they "encounter environments with the kinds of affordances they need to elaborate these prepared structures" (p. 476). Thus, when children play, the types of affordances provided by various play materials may also affect cognitive development.

Carr (2000) has suggested three affordance criteria that are useful for evaluating the action potentials of various play materials. These criteria are *transparency, challenge, and accessibility*. In relation to play materials, *transparency* refers to the quality of the material that enables the player to understand the concepts inherent in the toy or object. When a toy or other play material has transparency, the player does not need to guess or try various approaches in order to understand how to interact with that toy. For example, a jigsaw puzzle has immediate transparency because it signals to players how it should be used and provides feedback to the players as to whether their performance in placing the pieces is accurate. A technology–augmented toy or a computer program that signals the child's progress or success by triggering the toy's actions also would have transparency. Conversely, a toy or other play object that requires extensive guidance or training in order to play with it appropriately would have less transparency. Of course, transparency also differs in relation to the age and experience of the player since older or more experienced players may recognize transparency in more difficult puzzles or video games. Papert (1980) has indicated that perceiving the physical affordances of objects can lead to the creation of mental schemes or models that increase the transparency and extend it to other domains of understanding. That is, more complex objects can become transparent if the player already has mental schemes that can be related to that object.

Carr's second criterion, *challenge*, involves having affordances that increase the number of possibilities for action rather than narrowing the options to only a few actions. Some play materials, such as blocks and sand, have extensive possibilities for actions so they are high in challenge. A technology-augmented toy that requires only one type of reaction or interaction would have little challenge, but one that invites many interaction possibilities would have greater challenge. For example, a toy that makes the same sound each time one feature is pressed and that has no other manipulative devices would have low challenge, but if it makes a number of sounds that require varied responses by the child, it would have higher challenge, especially if different actions were required to produce each sound.

Carr's third characteristic, *accessibility*, is related to the amount and type of social participation that a toy affords. For example, a game that involves parent-child or peer collaboration would be judged to have greater accessibility than one that requires no social interaction. Some types of toy technologies afford extensive social participation while others allow only one participator and have no social contact possibilities. Certain play materials (e.g., puzzles) can be used in a solitary way or as a collaborative activity, but there are others (e.g., board games and baseball bats) that usually require other participants. In regard to technology-augmented play materials, some invite social participation and some do not, although even those that have solitary components often have the capability of interaction with other players in distant places. Thus, this method of gaining virtual accessibility through internet access can enhance this accessibility quality of the play material.

All three of these affordance qualities interface; for example, transparency is more likely to facilitate accessibility, and challenge is usually increased if the other two factors are present. In evaluating the effects of technology-augmented play materials, therefore, analysis of their affordances in comparison to the affordances of traditional play materials is an important requirement. As is true of all play materials, those that include technological augmentations may promote transparency, accessibility, and challenge or the augmentations may diminish such qualities. However, the context in which they are presented also plays a part in determining which representation modes can be elicited and the extent of the influence of the affordances of a play material.

Contexts

In regard to technology-augmented devices, an especially useful evaluative criterion is *context*. Context defines a setting, a circumstance, or the conditions present during an event or occurrence. It is important with respect to evaluation because it locates the evaluation within a frame in which other variables may have an impact. Without knowing the context, many questions are impossible to explore, and all evaluative results are incomplete. The general idea of context as it pertains to technology can be seen in the prior reflection on the definition of technology and in more practical examples such as the work done in defining context within content-aware computing (Dey, 2001; Dey, Abowd, & Salber, 2001). According to Dey and colleagues, information in both physical and electronic environments creates a context that affects the interaction between humans and computational services. They define context as information that characterizes entities that mediate the interaction between the user and the application. They state that context involves the "location, identity, and state of people, groups, and computational and physical objects" (p. 106) and indicate that every context involves interactions with "users, applications, and the surrounding environment" (p. 100).

The two major contextual categories of play with technological devices are defined as *physical* contexts and *virtual* contexts. These categories dominate the research landscape in reference to technology, primarily because of their flexibility and convenience. The distinction between physical and virtual is frequently seen in the literature on cyberbullying. For example, Patchin and Hinduja (2006) assert that technology can be implicated in the transmutation of bullying from the physical or real to the virtual or electronic. Similarly, Katzer, Fetchenhauer, and Belschak (2009) suggest that "bullying in internet chatrooms is not a phenomenon distinct from bullying in school. The primary difference lies in the context of action—virtuality vs. physical reality" (p. 32). Marsh (2010), however, states that play is primarily a social practice involving interactions with others and that this can occur "both in the virtual world and the physical world" (p. 32).

Physical and virtual contexts are generally accepted as different but not mutually exclusive constructs although there is some debate as to what exactly constitutes the two types of contexts. For example, Klahr et al. (2007) uses the phrase "real materials" (p. 185) to define the physical context and cites examples such as ramps, mechanical devices, and electronic items as real while limiting the virtual context to computer programs. Offermans and Hu (2013) add that the physical context (termed "world") includes sharing experiences with parents, the social context, physical activity, and physical behavior, while the virtual world is interactive, dynamic, tailored, fostering exploration and identity development, and affording unusual experiences. Burbules (2006) argues that "the key feature of the virtual context is not the type of technology that it produces but the sense of immersion itself" (p. 37). He suggests that virtual contexts are not passive simulated realities but active experiences in which the individuals' response and involvement create meaning. The "as-if" sense is maintained when the virtual experience is interesting and involving, engages the imagination, and is interactive.

In evaluating play experiences, Marsh (2010) noted that there is overlap between the physical and virtual categories and she suggests that technology advances may make these boundaries even more blurred. For example, she notes that although "rough and tumble play" is a term that typically describes physical wrestling and chasing, that term also can describe online play "that involved deliberate attempts by children to engage in avatar-to-avatar contact, including chasing and snowball fights, a form of play in which the majority of children interviewed reported having been involved" (p. 32). Klahr et al. (2007) agrees that virtual

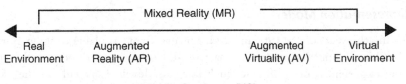

FIGURE 2.10 Mixed-Reality/Virtuality Continuum

materials can have a similar range of action as can occur when "physical materials are used in the real world" (p. 185). In both the physical and virtual context, children can remain in control of the materials being used. Marsh (2010) defines play as primarily a social practice involving interactions with others and that this can occur "in the virtual world and the physical world" (p. 32).

Milgram and Kishino (1994) proposed a taxonomy to discriminate between "real" and "virtual" and "mixed reality" venues. This "Virtual Continuum" describes two extremes "Real Environment" and "Virtual Environment," with "Mixed Reality" spanning these. Mixed Reality is composed of "Augmented Reality" and "Augmented Virtuality." Figure 2.10 shows this conceptualization.

In the taxonomy, Milgram and Kishino made three distinctions: 1) between real and virtual objects, 2) between direct and non-direct viewing, and 3) between real and virtual images. This taxonomy was designed to provide a framework that can unify seemingly disparate concepts and enable critical examination using common standards.

As technology advances, the contexts may continue to change. Within the analysis framework of this book, however, the term *physical* signifies real and tangible and *virtual* signifies mediation by technology-augmentation. This will enable readers to examine changes in the play landscape using this accessible perspective.

Representation Modes, Affordances, and Contexts of Traditional Toys

As technology has advanced over the centuries, these advances often have found expression in the toys and play of children. For example, during the industrial age, "mechanical" toys were available in a variety of forms and were usually activated when a button was pushed or a string was pulled. The toy actions, however, were relatively limited. A general look at toys in the 19th and 20th century reveal how certain representation modes and affordances were expressed, as well as the contextual environments in which the play occurred.

Representation Modes

During the years of the 19th and 20th centuries, toys available to the majority of children generally promoted enactive and iconic experiences, with symbolic experiences occurring at much later age levels. Especially in the early childhood years, the majority of toys involved enactive modes of interaction. For example, stacking blocks, push toys, balls, climbers, riding vehicles, and other toys for young children usually required the child to engage in many physical actions. Toys for older children also often encouraged motoric interactions. Elementary-age children used jump ropes, skates, climbers, bikes, and other toys requiring enactive responses. Iconic experiences were also common at later ages, with child use of dolls and action figures who engaged in child-enacted pretense scripts, and there were many toy props that encouraged pretend and language exploration. This pretense often involved symbolic modes as well, as language and writing were used to further the play scripts and the scenarios developed were often complex or of long duration. Thus, in play with traditional toys children would have had many opportunities to gain rich levels of cognitive understanding both through their initially physically enactive play and then later being engaged in play that involved iconic and symbolic levels of understanding. Play that embodied physical and motoric experiences provided the undergirding and visceral levels of understanding for the other representation modes. Also, many traditional modes of children's play provided integrated experiences that included enactive, iconic, and symbolic levels.

Affordances

Toys available to most children usually had high transparency because some toys were made by the child or a family member and resembled the activities in which the family engaged. For example, if a child made a dog from sticks, straw, and discarded cloth, the toy would be highly transparent because the qualities, components, and composition of the dog would be determined by the child. These types of toys, created by younger and older children based on their imaginations, would have high transparency because they were self-made. Manufactured toys and toys available to children from wealthier families would have high transparency if based on commonly available objects in the environment because they usually were simple enough for the child to understand the form and functions of the toy. Similarly, a manufactured wood-carved or cloth-sewed toy dog would still have high transparency because the child would be familiar with the qualities of a dog. Although the toy dog was not self-made, it would still be high in terms of transparency since the child would have had many experiences with real-world examples.

The challenge of such toys could be increased by the child simply adding or removing parts or accessories. The dog made from sticks, straw, and discarded cloth or the wooden or cloth manufactured dog toy might, on another day, be transformed by the child into a horse or some other animal. The nonprecise nature of the self-made toy would enable the child to make the toy to be anything that vaguely resembles a four-footed animal. A more exquisitely wood-carved dog, however, might have lower challenge because its precision would dictate its identity as a dog. Still, it could be many types of dog and the child also might imagine it to be a horse or other animal, but it is more likely that the child would stay with the manufacturer's toy label. In the case of both the child-made and the manufactured dogs, however, the child could make changes such as adding some wings made of leaves, and then imagine the toy to be a flying animal. For less defined manufactured toys, such as blocks, children always could play at many levels of challenge. This is one reason that blocks have been such a long-lasting favorite with children because they could be used in many ways.

The accessibility of early toys might vary because children could play alone or with others and many toys, such as balls, were enhanced by group participation. The self-made and manufactured dogs, for example, might be played with alone but could also be part of a pretend world designed by siblings or friends, in which that toy interacted with others. Games with balls usually would have high accessibility, allowing a number of children to play simultaneously. Throwing a ball at a target bottle might involve turn-taking or developing rules for a more elaborate game. Ball play usually has high accessibility because it readily lends itself to group play. Other toys, for example board games, required multiple participants and thus they also had high accessibility. Thus, in general many early toys had the quality of high accessibility because they required multiple participants by virtue of their nature and design. Even if multiple participants were not required, the option to play with others while using the toy was entirely the child's choice. A jump rope is another example of a toy that has high accessibility although there is an individual element to its use. In this case, the individual can play alone and keep score by counting the number of consecutive jumps. Group play is also possible and it may be turn-based, such as a competition to see who can make the most consecutive jumps, or it can involve everyone with two individuals swinging the rope and the other children taking turns jumping.

In the 21st century, these affordance possibilities are still evident in non-technology-augmented toys. Such toys that have withstood the test of time—for example, the jump rope and wooden blocks—still have the same affordances as they did hundreds of years ago. Their purpose is transparent, they can be used simply or in complex ways, and they promote individual or group play. Similar to earlier times, however, there are significant differences between toys depending on their cost. More expensive toys are usually more complex, highly refined, and generally have more features and accessories. Whether these accessories and features promote transparency, challenge, and accessibility, however, or restrain some of these play opportunities is a question of interest.

For example, the initial design of toys such as Legos allowed children to create objects limited only by the child's imagination. In terms of affordances, the basic blocks have high transparency because their shape dictates how they can be connected. They have very high challenge because they can be assembled into a variety of shapes with different implied functions. They also have high accessibility, because there is nothing inherent in the blocks that prevent group play. However, the affordances of these blocks change significantly when the blocks are designed for a specific purpose. For example, many of these blocks now come in kits that suggest they be assembled to a predetermined shape with predetermined functions. The child still could create other shapes, of course, but this requires overcoming the explicit message of the predetermined shape and structures that are "supposed" to be constructed. In this case, transparency remains high because the blocks contain all information necessary for their use. Challenge, however, is reduced because interaction with the toy is now limited to assembling the blocks into the predetermined state and then interacting with the finished produced in a manner consistent with the design. Accessibility remains somewhat the same, because there is nothing inherent in the toy that prevents the child from playing with others.

Contexts

The examination of contexts of play in earlier times presents a picture that is very different from the context issues that have arisen with the advent of technology-augmented play objects. Play in earlier times usually involved contexts that would be identified as *physical*. During the mid-20th century, however, some *virtual* contexts began to be available. For example, programs heard on the radio sometimes encouraged some game-like play. Evaluation of play materials becomes more difficult when the *virtual* and *mixed-reality* contexts are considered. Although for young children, physical types of play materials continue to predominate, because play objects and their features now have become so complex, it is sometimes difficult to separate the physical, virtual, and mixed conditions. Many present-day technology-augmented play materials had origins in early play objects such as doll figures, transportation vehicles, and construction materials, but their virtual capabilities have increased tremendously over the past few years. With the advent of *video games* and *online play environments* in the late 20th century, the distinctions among these context differences are more difficult to separate because they reflect the reality of present-day *mixed-reality* play.

Potential Effects of the Changing Play Landscape

Play materials in the past clearly were differentiated in regard to their representation modes, their affordances, and their contexts. However, there have been many changes in the play environment, especially in the last 50 years, and the substance of the representation modes, affordance characteristics, and context environments have changed as well. The current trends in play that are increasing the pervasiveness and complexity of technology-augmentation in both traditional and innovative play materials appear to be changing the landscape of play for both children and adolescents. Whether these differences in the play experiences of children and adolescents will result in differences in brain development and subsequently in social, emotional, moral, and cognitive development is presently only at the level of speculation. However, since play often provides the environment for growth in these other developmental areas, this question is an important one to consider.

FIGURE 2.11 The snow is fun to play in!

FIGURE 2.12 We're driving like dad does.

FIGURE 2.13 See me make a splash in the pool!

FIGURE 2.14 I am learning to ride my new bike.

Activities and Questions for Discussion

1. Select two of your favorite toys or games from early or later childhood and analyze what representation modes and affordances they provided that made them enjoyable. What were their context characteristics and how did they affect the play?
2. As an adolescent or adult, what are two of your favorite play (or leisure!) activities? Describe the representation modes, affordances, and context characteristics of these play materials.
3. Read one research article that analyzes some type of technology-augmented play material and write a paragraph stating how the researchers studied the play, the type of data they collected, and their conclusions about the effects of this type of play on some aspect of human development. Even if they did not discuss representation modes, affordances or contexts, suggest how these criteria may have affected their results.

References

American Academy of Pediatrics. (2001). Children, adolescents, and television. *Pediatrics, 107*(2), 423.

American Academy of Pediatrics (2013). Children, adolescents, and the media. *Pediatrics, 132*(5), 958–961.

Bergen, D. (2003, November). *College students' memories of their childhood play: A ten year comparison.* Paper presentation at the annual conference of the National Association for the Education of Young Children, Chicago.

Bergen, D., Liu, W., & Liu, G. (1997). Chinese and American students' memories of childhood play: A comparison. *International Journal of Educology, 1*(2), 109–127.

Bergen, D., & Williams, E. (2008). *Differing childhood play experiences of young adults compared to earlier young adult cohorts have implications for physical, social, and academic development.* Poster presentation at the annual meeting of the Association for Psychological Science, Chicago, IL.

Bruner, J.S. (1964). The course of cognitive growth. *American Psychologist, 19*(1), 1–15.

Burbules, N.C. (2006). Rethinking the virtual. In J. Weiss, J. Nolan, J. Hunsinger, & P. Trifonas (Eds.), *The international handbook of virtual learning environments* (Vol. 1, pp. 37–58). Dordrecht, The Netherlands: Springer.

Carr, M. (2000). Technological affordances, social practice and learning narratives in an early childhood setting. *International Journal of Technology and Design Education, 10*, 61–79.

Davis, D., & Bergen, D. (2014). Relationships among play behaviors reported by college students and their responses to moral issues: A pilot study. *Journal of Research in Childhood Education, 28*, 484–498.

Davis, D., & Bergen, D. (2015). *College students' technology-related play reports show differing gender and age patterns.* Poster presentation at the Association for Psychological Science, New York.

Dey, A.K. (2001). Understanding and using context. *Human-Computer Interaction Institute*. Paper 34. http://repository.cmu.edu/hcii/34

Dey, A.K., Abowd, G.D., & Salber, D. (2001). A conceptual framework and a toolkit for supporting the rapid prototyping of context-aware applications. *Human-Computer Interaction, 16,* 97–166.

Erdogan, N., Corlu, M.S., & Capraro, R.M. (2013). Defining innovation literacy: Do robotics programs help students develop innovation literacy skills? *International Online Journal of Educational Sciences, 5*(1), 1–9.

Gardner, H., & Davis, K. (2013). *The app generation: How today's youth navigate identity, intimacy, and imagination in a digital world.* Yale University Press.

Gibson, E.J. (1969). *Principles of perceptual learning and development.* New York: Appleton-Century-Crofts.

Goldstein, J.H. (2013). Technology and play. *Scholarpedia, 8*(2), 304–334.

Jenkins, H. (2009). *Confronting the challenges of participatory culture: Media education for the 21st century.* MIT Press.

Kafai, Y. (2006). Play and technology: Revised realities and potential perspectives. In D.P. Fromberg & D. Bergen (Eds.), *Play from birth to twelve: Contexts, perspectives, and meanings* (2nd ed., pp. 207–214). New York: Routledge.

Kahn, P.H., Friedman, B., Perez-Granados, D.R., & Freier, N.G. (2004). *Robotic pets in the lives of preschool children.* Paper presented at CHI, Vienna, Austria, April.

Kang, C. (2013, December 10). Infant iPad seats raise concerns about screen time for babies, http://www.washingtonpost.com/business/economy/fisher-prices-infant-ipad-seat-raises-concerns-about-baby-screen-time/2013/12/10/6ebba48e-61bb-11e3-94ad-004fefa61ee6_story.html

Katzer, C., Fetchenhauer, D., & Belschak, F. (2009). Cyberbullying: Who are the victims?: A comparison of victimization in internet chatrooms and victimization in school. *Journal of Media Psychology: Theories, Methods, and Applications, 21*(1), 25.

Klahr, D., Triona, L.M., & Williams, C. (2007). Hands on what? The relative effectiveness of physical versus virtual materials in an engineering design project by middle school children. *Journal of Research in Science Teaching, 44*(1), 183–203.

Levin, D. (2013). *Beyond remote-controlled childhood: Teaching young children in the media age.* Washington, DC: NAEYC.

Lim, S.S., & Clark, L.S. (2010). Virtual worlds as a site of convergence for children's play. *Journal For Virtual Worlds Research, 3*(2), 1–19.

Marsh, J. (2010). Young children's play in online virtual worlds. *Journal of Early Childhood Research, 8*(1), 23–39.

Milgram, P., & Kishino, F. (1994). A taxonomy of mixed reality visual displays. *IEICE TRANSACTIONS on Information and Systems, 77*(12), 1321–1329.

Offermans, S., & Hu, J. (2013). Augmenting a virtual world game in a physical environment. *Journal of Man, Machine and Technology, 2*(1), 54–62.

Papert, S. (1980). *Mindstorms.* Brighton, MA: Harvester.

Patchin, J.W., & Hinduja, S. (2006). Bullies move beyond the schoolyard: A preliminary look at cyberbullying. *Youth Violence and Juvenile Justice, 4*(2), 148–169.

Plowman, L., Stevenson, O., Stephen, C., & McPake, J. (2012). Preschool children's learning with technology at home. *Computers & Education, 59*(1), 30–37.

Resnick, L.B. (1994). Situated rationalism: Biological and social preparation for learning. In L.A. Hirschfeld & S.A. Gelman (Eds.), *Mapping the mind.* Cambridge, UK: University of Cambridge.

Wartella, E., Caplovitz, A.G., & Lee, J.H. (2004). From Baby Einstein to Leapfrog, from Doom to the Sims, from instant messaging to internet chat rooms: Public interest in the role of interactive media in children's lives. *Social Policy Report, 28*(4), 1–19.

Weigel, D.J., Martin, S.S., & Bennett, K. K. (2010). Pathways to literacy: Connections between family assets and preschool children's emergent literacy skills. *Journal of Early Childhood Research, 8*(1), 5–22.

3

POTENTIAL INFLUENCES OF REPRESENTATION MODES AND AFFORDANCES ON VARIOUS TYPES OF TECHNOLOGY-AUGMENTED PLAY

Gains and Losses

Jeannette doesn't mind taking long trips with her children, Bill (age 10) and Mary (age 7) because they rarely complain about the boring nature of the trip. Jeanette remembers the way trips used to be with her parents when they took the children to visit relatives in another state. Although they had coloring books and magnetic board games, they soon tired of those so their parents played games with them like "find all the letters of the alphabet on road signs" or "count how many animals you see" in order to keep the children engaged during the long ride. Her dad sang old time songs and the kids would make up songs. Sometimes her mom would ask easy math problems to see who could get the answer fastest. They also stopped at a few parks along the way so everyone could run around. Now Jeannette can just relax and think her own thoughts during the drive with her children since they have their iPads and iPhone apps to keep them occupied the entire time.

The toy designers, developmental theorists, and researchers who have predicted positive or negative effects of technology-augmented play materials often focus on one or two aspects of the toy or virtual product to make their predictions about the potential effects of play with those products. This may be why they have such varied perceptions of the value of these play materials. Using the criteria based on representation modes, affordances, and contexts may be useful for increasing the readers' ability to understand the potential effects of various technology-augmented play materials. Although these play materials are continuing to change and expand exponentially, one way to categorize and evaluate them is by focusing on their context and intended age group. The contexts may be physical or virtual, and the virtual context can be further divided into digital games and online play environments. Technology-augmented play materials also can be described for three age levels: infants, toddlers and preschoolers; elementary-age children; and adolescents. There are examples of playthings in both contexts and at all age levels, but some types predominate at certain age levels. For example, robotic human or animal figures that are programmed to "talk" or act in certain ways are very common playthings for toddlers and preschoolers. Video games, however, are most pervasive in the play of elementary-age children and adolescents. Virtual materials such as smart phone apps are available for all age levels and some are even designed for pets (e.g., Friskies Jitterbug)!

Physical Context Play

Play materials within the physical context are concrete, tangible, and have physical dimensions and properties. Traditional materials for play have usually involved children in much engagement with physical contexts. Some of this play occurred with simply manufactured toys or even homemade toys and even included naturally occurring materials such as sticks or sand. Also, play usually included other children or their pets and the sessions often involved elaborated pretense scripts. For example, children might use stones and wood to build a "house" and then make a "bed" of grass in which they would place their "baby" (their kitten). Sometimes children would invent a game of "stick ball" and use the boundaries of the yard as the playing field. Much play occurred outdoors in natural settings such as parks or streets or in the basements or backyards of homes, and the play often lasted for extended periods. Thus, play within the physical context often involved extensive interaction with the natural world. At the present time, although many children still use play materials such as blocks, balls, dolls, and toy cars, many of these traditional toys now also come in technology-augmented versions. Such technology-augmented toys are particularly popular for infants, toddlers, and preschoolers. Young children today also have the option and ability to engage in play with games, stories, and videos via devices that are primarily for adult use. These play opportunities blur the line between the physical and virtual context because they require a physical means to control virtual actions.

Physical Context Play for Young Children

Although some technology-augmented toys for young children have been available since the late 20th century (see Bergen, 2001), such play materials for infants, toddlers, and preschoolers have increased exponentially in the past few

years. An example of a very popular toy with a technology-augmented component is Tickle Me Elmo™, which was initially marketed in the mid-1990s. This
is a plush toy with a computer chip that causes the toy to giggle, shake, and finally
laugh wildly when it is squeezed a number of times. Many other commonly
used toys have had technology-augmented components added. For example,
the original Fisher-Price Little People™ toys in the 1950s were mechanical in
nature and did not have electronic components. The current versions of the toys,
however, have integrated technology that play audio and control simple actions.
There has also been an increase in the complexity of toy actions for children,
and even toys that could "speak" and perform simple actions have been replaced
by more complex toys such as the AIBO™ dog, which was introduced in the
late 1990s, and the more recent ZOOMER™. In both cases, the toys have sensors and motors that allow them to interact with the environment and provide
responses consistent with their real-world counterparts, dogs. Complexity in
modern toys is perhaps best exemplified by the new "systems" that are available
for children in this age group. Systems or platforms such as Leapfrog's Leap
Reader Books™ and the even more complex LeapFrog LeapPad3 Power
Learning Tablet™ could easily pass for adult devices based on the amount of
technology they contain and their extensive capabilities. These toys are marketed
as all-in-one systems that both entertain and enhance the learning and development of young children.

Presently a high proportion of toys for young children now have some
technology-augmented components. These toys give directions to children
and suggest themes for play. Many of them simulate the talk and actions of living creatures or media figures. This play often occurs in solitary environments
(bedrooms) or in closely structured environments (after-school classes). Thus,
the physical contexts of child play have been changed or augmented by many
aspects of technology. Virtual worlds were not a traditional focus of marketing
to young children, but because many young children have access to their parents' technology-augmented devices and apps, the virtual context has become
extremely important.

Physical Context Play for Elementary-Age Children

Technology-augmented toy play for elementary-age children is differentiated
from play at earlier ages primarily by the complexity of the toys. This is most
likely due to the fact that, as compared to younger children, elementary-age
children have increased motor skill development, verbal abilities, and a greater
understanding of concepts such as cause and effect. With these developmental
advances, elementary-age children are able to perform more complex tasks and,
more importantly, they have increased abilities to make meaning from their play
experiences. Technology-augmented toys at this age range from less complex

dolls or figures that play audio or perform simple tasks to more sophisticated robotic playthings that are characterized by humanoid or non-humanoid figures that can perform a wide array of actions. One example of a complex toy at this age is WowWee's Robosapien X Robot™, which features full arm and gripper movement, realistic walking and running, and sensors that allow it to respond to the environment. Although the Robosapien X has basic user-controlled functions, it is considered advanced because of its ability to be programmed. Radio-controlled toys are another class of modern plaything prevalent at this age and these may be realistic representations of actual vehicles or simply advanced machines with unusual designs. One example of a popular radio-controlled vehicle that requires increased motor function is the Syma S107™ 3-channel radio-controlled helicopter. Although this toy features a gyroscope for stable flight, basic control of the toy requires skills beyond those of younger children.

Physical Context Play for Adolescents

Adolescents generally have more developed fine motor skills and coordination than elementary-age children. At this stage, they seek to define and differentiate themselves from others. Physical, social, and cognitive developmental changes parallel the shifts in play opportunities that adolescents seek and also how they experience play. Consequently, adolescents' advanced abilities are often reflected in their choices of toys at this age. The types of playthings used by adolescents typically include some used by younger children, but in general the toys are more complex in nature. Complexity in this case does not only refer to technological complexity, but it also includes complexity in terms of themes and content. Non-technology playthings that offer increased complexity in terms of themes include board games such as chess, and card games such as Magic: the Gathering™ and Cards Against Humanity™. These games require players to formulate strategies, solve problems, and in the case of Cards Against Humanity, the player must navigate complex adult themes within the game and among the other players of the game. Technology-augmented toys at this age are similar to those from earlier ages, with the addition of complex features and capabilities. For example, the Syma S107 3-channel radio-controlled helicopter would give way to the 8-channel DJI Phantom 2 Vision+ Quadcopter™. In both cases, the toys have significant motor skill requirements, but this quadcopter has advanced requirements for control of the both the basic movements of the toy and manipulation of its picture and video capabilities. Features such as the programmable flight path require the user to be familiar with the toy as well as other technologies including common mobile devices. More importantly, however, the capabilities of this quadcopter have features related to image and video capture that may force users to navigate complex issues such as the balance between personal freedom and the privacy and security of others.

Common Themes Occurring in Technology-Augmented Play Materials

Several general themes emerge when examining modern technology-augmented playthings across the different ages: complexity, fidelity, and control. Complexity in toys appears to increase as the target age increases. Generally, toys at earlier ages tend to rely on a limited number of skills and they tend to have fewer requirements for manipulation. This is expected given that most toys target a certain age range and are thus designed to be developmentally appropriate for that age range. One example that illustrates increasing complexity as age increases is Legos. Infants, toddlers, and preschoolers can play with Lego Duplo bricks, which do not generally contain technological enhancements, and are twice the length, width, and height of regular Lego bricks. Elementary-age children can select themed Lego sets including Star Wars, Technics, and Disney Princess. These sets are intricate and they may be technologically augmented with motors and sensors to perform specific tasks. Adolescents have many Lego options including Fusion, which combines the physical block building with virtual games and representations on smartphones or mobile devices, and Mindstorms, where players can create robotic playthings from intricate blocks.

Fidelity or realism also increases in parallel with age. Although some dolls or figures at early ages have realistic appearances, the realistic capabilities of toys generally increase with the age of the player. For example, the AIBO or the DJI quadcopter both have increased fidelity in terms of functions and capabilities as compared to the stuffed dog or the play helicopter used by the toddler. This phenomenon is expected as it is also an indication of increasing complexity as age increases. Control also changes with age. Toys designed for manual manipulation are replaced by toys that are controlled remotely via specific controls or via smart devices. Interestingly, as young children increasingly use smart devices, the complexity, fidelity, and control become blurred as young children are exposed to play scenarios with extremely realistic representations. As this change occurs, it is reasonable to question the long-term effects in an effort to determine consequences of changes in play, especially given the increasing complexity of toys for young children.

Representation Modes and Affordances in Physical Context Play

The representation modes and affordances of technology-augmented play materials within the physical context differ in a number of respects from those typically present in such play in previous generations. Although there is great variation depending on the design of the toy, in general many of these toys often make the child the "reactor" rather than the "actor" (Bergen, 2001). That is, the toy directs the play rather than the child. This also appears to be the case when considering changing play patterns from infants to adolescents. Modern play with technology-augmented materials becomes more centered on the toy and its capabilities, and less on what the individual brings to the experience. This pattern appears to be accelerating as complexity increases via advances in technology and as toys become more specialized.

Representation Modes

One change that is clear in modern toys is that the *enactive* mode of cognitive understanding, which involves motor responses, is not as evident in play with many technology-augmented toys. For example, young children primarily use their fingers to connect virtual blocks instead of using their whole body in actions that are common activities in play with wooden blocks such as holding, carrying, picking up, balancing, and knocking down. Both preschool and elementary-age children spend more time operating the various toy features and observing the toy's actions, and many times the action is a replay of media plots rather than engagement in spontaneously designed unique plots created by the children. Although the *enactive* mode is not as common, the *iconic* and *symbolic* levels are pervasive in technology-augmented play materials, and usually present the toy designer's view of what the "real" world is like.

The design of the toys often exaggerates features or behaviors so that the picture of the world that is presented (*iconic*) and the meaning of the actions and language (*symbolic*) may not accurately represent the "real"-world experiences. The changes are evident at all age levels and they are particularly visible when children use complex and feature-rich toys. Even with its stimulating array of software options, for example, LeapFrog's LeapPad3 Power Learning Tablet requires only that the child hold the device in the prescribed manner and press the buttons with predefined functions. The same is true for the Robosapien at the elementary-age level, and the DJI quadcopter at the adolescent level. In all cases, there is an overemphasis on the iconic and symbolic, and an underutilization and appreciation of the importance of the enactive mode.

While different toys may have differing levels of representation, the general trend is that modern toys, to a large degree, incorporate technologies that perform the actions that the player traditionally performed. This transfer of both action and causes of action from the child to the toy results in less opportunity for the child to be the one creating or enacting. Designers of some toys attempt, purposefully or not, to balance this shift of responsibility by introducing iconic and symbolic elements that are in many instances very exaggerated. For example, the soldier's battle cry is always loud even when in "stealth-mode." Thus, the child's ability to affect the quality of the interactions becomes more limited.

Affordances

The transparency, challenge, and accessibility of technology-augmented play materials may vary greatly, depending on the toy design and usage characteristics.

The toy may be high in transparency if the toy "tells" the child exactly what to do but low in challenge if there are only a few actions that can be taken. The toy may be high in challenge initially but be less challenging later if only repetitive actions are permitted. The toy may promote accessibility for play with other children or require an individual child's focus such that playmates are not required.

The affordances of many toys for infants, toddlers, and preschoolers have changed over time, but the magnitude of the changes depends on what toys are considered. For example, the current toy product Lego Duplo has high transparency because the blocks signal where and how they might be connected, they have high challenge because they can be combined to create unlimited new playthings to suit various scenarios, and they have high accessibility because they easily allow cooperative play with other children. The simplicity of this non-technology-augmented toy mirrors toys from previous generations; thus, there are few changes in terms of the richness of affordances in that example. Many current technology-augmented toys, however, are very different from toys of previous generations in terms of affordances. They may share similar themes, but the technology component introduces new variables that must be considered. For example, the Tickle Me Elmo doll is thematically similar to dolls from previous generations, but there are small differences in affordances due to the technological capabilities of the new toy. The transparency remains similar because the doll itself signals many of the ways that it can be used, and most children discover the audio capabilities of the doll very quickly. Thus, the transparency is minimally affected by the doll's technology-augmented component. Accessibility is also similar because Tickle Me Elmo can be easily shared, although turn-taking will be an issue at early ages. However, this was also the case with toys from previous generations.

Arguably, challenge is most affected in this case for a number of reasons. Tickle Me Elmo has added features that previous dolls did not possess and this means that it provides one more dimension through which interaction can occur. In this scenario, challenge is increased because the technology embedded in the doll adds one more potential for interaction. On the other hand, the presence of the technology can reduce challenge because it signals one predominant way that interaction should occur. For example, Tickle Me Elmo signals that it should be tickled. While it is possible to interact with the doll in unlimited ways, the presence of the technology provides implicit boundaries that "guide" how the child should play with the toy. Because the same sound is repeated, the toy decreases in challenge after continuing play. There is nothing stopping the child from pretending that Elmo is a superhero, but that would require the child to act in a way contrary to the toy's signals.

Complex toy systems such as Fisher-Price Laugh and Learn™ and LeapFrog's LeapPad3 Power Learning Tablet have comparability to some toys from previous generations, but their technology-augmented affordances have become a prevalent part of the play experiences of younger children. In only a few years, these systems have evolved from simple systems with a few capabilities and features, to the current highly complex and feature-rich systems. Examining the affordances of these systems illustrates how they are changing the nature of play for children. Looking at transparency, these systems are relatively transparent because they are designed such that the children can immediately begin interacting. Advanced features may require adult explanation or help from a knowledgeable peer, but basic operation is, for the most part, intuitive. These systems signal how they are to be used and factors such as the placement of controls and buttons are the result of years of research in human and machine interaction. Challenge is an interesting affordance in that at first glance it might seem that the toy has high challenge because there are unlimited actions that can be taken when interacting with the toy's software. However, it can also be argued that challenge is low despite the numerous software-driven interactions because the hardware only allows the user to interact via a limited collection of buttons with defined functions. Within this perspective, it is questionable that these systems build traits such as imagination and creativity. Even when the software presents a free space to design or create, the child is constrained by the specifications of the device. In regard to creativity, the child might be better served with a box of crayons and a sheet of paper! Examining accessibility is also very difficult because at first glance, these systems provide a network that allows children to play together if others have similar devices. The issue is summarized by the question "What does group play look like?" A typical scenario would have a group of children, each of whom possesses a device, playing together via the system, but not necessarily speaking to or directly interacting with each other. Are the children playing together? These complex networked systems increase the likelihood that group play changes to individual play, albeit within a shared space.

Modern technology-augmented toys for elementary age children have features never seen in previous generations, and these may have differential effects on the toys' affordances. For example the Robosapien robots have moderate to high transparency for today's children because the basic functions of the toy are easily grasped during initial interaction. More advanced features, however, may require assistance. Challenge is low for this type of toy because although the toy has many capabilities, its design for the most part determines how it should be used. Similar to toys for younger children, toys like the Robosapien robots do not necessarily prevent a child from scripting play differently from what the designers intended, but in all probability, children will most often use the toy similarly to its designed purpose. Accessibility is interesting for the Robosapien robots because while two children can watch and interact with the toy simultaneously, only one child can control the toy at any time. In many ways, the affordances of technology-augmented toys for elementary-age children are similar to those for infants, toddlers, and preschoolers. Differences that exist in accessibility may be the result of the assumption that play is more individualized at the elementary age.

The affordances of technology-augmented toys for adolescents are similar to those for elementary-aged children, with small exceptions for transparency and accessibility. In terms of transparency, most toys are intuitive, but the more advanced toys like the DJI Phantom 2 Vision+ quadcopter may require planning or assistance for even the most basic functions. The challenge affordance is similar to the other ages, where in some cases, the toys dictate the play and the child is explicitly or implicitly limited in making changes to the play script. Accessibility, similar to that at elementary age, remains moderate because these toys do not foster group play outside the scenario where either each child takes a turn, or each child must have the toy, and in the latter case, play is potentially individual although in a group setting.

Virtual Context Play

Within the theoretical framework of this book, play material in the virtual context are all mediated by technology-augmentation, meaning that interaction occurs via a technology-augmented medium. The virtual context can be divided into two areas: Digital Games and Online Play Environments. These two areas are not exhaustive, but they are useful starting points through which technology-augmented play materials can be examined.

Digital Games

When considering the technology-augmented world of children, perhaps the most dominant and notable influence can be seen in areas of digital gaming, while the type of technology through which children play in digital games shapes the nature of the play. As such, it is important to consider digital gaming for children by examining the affordances, representations, and constraints of the technology through with children play digital games as well as the nature of the games themselves. These three factors exert influence on the rapidly evolving landscape of the technology-augmented world for children and have implications on the brain development processes in a variety of ways.

There are multiple ways to classify digital games and these classifications may focus on characteristics such as the nature of the game play (e.g., action, adventure, role-playing, puzzle, strategy), the perspective of the play (e.g., first-person, third-person), the visual representation of game worlds (e.g., 2D, 3D), and the purpose of the game (e.g., educational, training, exercise, casual, serious). While each of these classification taxonomies may be useful in categorizing games, in order to better understand the ways in which digital gaming influences the brain development of children, these various characteristics of games function as attributes that may have different influences on brain development processes. Much like the way that children alternate through different styles of real-world play, they are also likely to alternate through various games in which the nature of game play differs. A child may develop an affinity for a particular genre of games and explore various games with similar game play. This same child may then progress through multiple genres of games depending on factors such as availability of technology, requisite motor skills, and presence or absence of other children. Given that there are many types of digital games and that they can be classified in numerous ways, this section first discusses digital games via the lens of common devices, then selects types of popular games at the various age levels, before examining the representation modes and affordances of digital games. Most games can be played on multiple systems and devices and many games cross various boundaries used for categorization.

The world of digital gaming is rapidly changing and is influenced largely by advances in technology hardware. Advances that lead to lower production costs, improved power efficiency, and additional functionality in consumer devices are quickly integrated into new game development an increasingly rapid pace. For example, advances that enabled touch-sensitive interfaces to become commonplace on mobile devices have made a touch-based interface a commonplace control interface for mobile games, whereas previous game development would rely on an dedicated control interface such as a button controller or joystick. In this case, the technological advances were rapidly integrated into game play for existing game genres while also sparking the development of entirely new genres of games for which the touch-based interface was essential. With significant changes in the physical interaction, as well as new forms of games that were not previously possible, it is reasonable to expect that these changes would lead to differences in motor skill development, hand-eye coordination, and other developmental processes that are influenced by games and that are ongoing throughout childhood and adolescence.

Although these technological advances are rapidly evolving, digital games typically are played through specific devices, and these devices are unique in their affordances and constraints for game play. When considered broadly, digital games are most commonly played in one of three types of devices: gaming consoles, personal computers, or mobile devices. Gaming consoles, such as Xbox™, are usually home-based devices that are attached to a television or other video display. Historically, gaming consoles were designed for the primary purpose of playing digital games; however, more recent gaming consoles are multifunction devices that enable game play, video entertainment, and internet-based communication functionality. The specific gaming functionality provided by a gaming console differs by manufacturer. A notable difference in gaming consoles is in the ways in which a user can interact with the gaming console and thus interact within the game as well. For example, early gaming consoles relied on joystick or button controllers for interaction while current gaming consoles use more advanced interaction controls that may be joystick or button controls as well as interaction through motion-sensing controllers and sensors as well as voice control. Elmo's Musical Monsterpiece™ is an example of a console game for infants, toddlers, and preschoolers. This adventure game for the Nintendo DS™, 3Ds™, and Wii™, introduces children to music and the basics of making music.

Although the functionality of a personal computer (PC) with respect to digital gaming is very similar to that of a gaming console in that PCs are multipurpose devices, PC-based games were early to take advantage of connectivity and mobility. The physical interaction with a personal computer is more commonly facilitated through the use of a keyboard, mouse controls, or connected gaming controller. As such, the interaction within PC-based games has led to a rise in hardware developed specifically to facilitate game play. Gaming keyboards or mouse controls offer specific advantages for genres of games such as first-person games that require players to navigate a virtual world. Also, the mobility afforded by laptop computers and the continual expansion of wireless networking has made a laptop computer a portable gaming console that can be distinctly different than either the gaming consoles described previously or the mobile devices that are described later. Although the degree to which children have access to a personal computer is unclear, the availability of personal computers in homes and schools suggests that many children have access to these devices; thus, it is likely that they are also part of the digital gaming landscape for many children as well. One example is the Halo™ series published by Microsoft and available on consoles and PCs. The violent first-person shooter, appropriate for adolescents, casts the player in the role of Master Chief John-117 who must save humanity from the alien enemies.

Mobile devices for digital gaming have been available for nearly as long as gaming consoles have been marketed. Beginning with handheld electronic games that were single-purpose devices that played only one game and featured controls unique to that game, later devices such as the Nintendo DS featured changeable game cartridges and functioned as handheld gaming consoles similar to their home-based counterparts. More recent innovations that have led to the near ubiquity of smartphones and mobile tablets have arguably had the most notable influence on digital gaming especially for elementary-age children.

Although smartphones and tablets are distinct in many ways, with respect to digital gaming, their functionality is largely similar; thus, it is reasonable to consider mobile phones and tablets more generally as a category of technology-augmented devices. Within this category, multiple factors account for a rise in digital gaming on mobile devices by elementary-age and even younger children, beginning with cost, size, and functionality. Also, the cost of mobile devices has dramatically decreased, thus making the devices themselves more widely adopted. The small size of mobile devices have made them easily portable and also usable by children and their multipurpose nature also make them essential for adults to use for a wide variety of purposes, including communication, entertainment, real-world navigation, and information-seeking. The sheer ubiquity of these devices has also yielded a new market of software for these devices that features games and "apps," for example Angry Birds™ and Candy Crush Saga™, that are free, low-cost, or supported by advertisement revenue. All of these factors function together to create an environment in which children have access to mobile devices at a rate that is much higher than any other category of device, at a lower cost, and in nearly any type of location.

In addition to the environmental changes that have led to greater access to mobile devices, the nature of interaction that is unique to mobile devices also enhances their appeal to children. A touch-based interface and motion-sensing interaction enabled by miniaturized accelerometers and gyroscopes within the devices have made these devices more intuitive for children to use than they often are for adults who have more experience with earlier interface designs that use controls separate from the visual display. Although the limited buying power of children suggests that they may have not been the primary market when these devices were first developed, the frequent use of these devices by children continues to influence the market of both the mobile hardware and software, including digital gaming for mobile devices.

Categories of Digital Game Play for Children

Within the various categories of digital games, it is reasonable to assume that there are children who play games in most, if not all, categories of digital games. However, there are specific games and game genres that offer unique perspectives on how various digital games have become part of a child's developmental experience.

Simulation Games

The category of simulation games is wide-ranging and includes games that simulate a real-world place or activity. In a typical role-playing simulation for children, players are controlling various aspects of a virtual space that may simulate a real-world business, such as virtual pet shop, hair salon, or restaurant. Among the games that are in this category are those that simulate living organisms such as Pets for the Playstation Vita, and also games that simulate a common activity, such as Toca Hair Salon 2™; both games are for toddlers. The complexity of these games ranges from simple tactile interaction such as using virtual scissors to cut hair to action as complex as controlling multiple aspects of a virtual business in order to reach a higher level of achievement. Many of these games are developed specifically as apps for mobile devices or handheld consoles, although some games are available for gaming consoles and personal computers. One of the most popular and complex simulation games is The Sims™ series. This game, suitable for adolescents, allows players to simulate human life within a virtual world that is complete with other virtual people. Players must manage everything from the health of their Sim to the daily interactions and emotions associated with the Sim's virtual life.

Platform Action Games

Platform action games are those in which a virtual player is controlled by the user through a series of obstacles, obstructions, or other types of actions that require a combination of basic actions such as jumping and running. Some games in this category have a history as long as gaming consoles themselves have existed and they have evolved into a series of games featuring the same characters or narrative storyline. One notable aspect of these games is that the virtual player often has a set number of "lives" and the user controls the player until the virtual player "dies." Older examples of these types of games are Super Mario Brothers™, which is a side-scrolling interface controlled by a player via a dedicated button-based controller, while newer examples in this category are "endless running" games such as the Subway Surfers™ series or new releases in the Tomb Raider™ series in which a character is continually running and the user controls the avatar to navigate obstacles and collect virtual coins.

Sandbox Games

As a general category, sandbox games are those that provide a virtual space for creation, experimentation, building, and similar activities. However, there are many sandbox games that may offer game-play modes that fall into other categories as well. Perhaps one of the most popular games within this category is Minecraft™, which is suitable for the elementary-age child and the adolescent. In this game, the user has a first-person view of a virtual world in which they can play in multiple game modes including creative, survival, or adventure modes. Within the virtual world, a user controls various tools and objects to interact with the world to construct or demolish virtual objects. Minecraft is considered an "open-world" game in which there is no predefined objective for the user to achieve and the user may choose to play in any one of the modes available. In creative mode, a player may choose to build objects or structures in the virtual world, whereas survival mode introduces additional requirements that require the player to gather resources needed for survival and other constraint or threats to the players "health" such as monsters that emerge at night. Adventure mode is similar to survival mode, but with the ability for users to follow predetermined maps and adventures developed by other players. Minecraft can be played by a single user, or in a multiuser environment in which players are interacting in a common virtual world from separate devices connected via a network connection.

Massively Multiplayer Online Games

Massively Multiplayer Online (MMO) games support many simultaneous users playing within a virtual world. The virtual worlds are usually thematic, for example fantasy worlds or space-based worlds, and players compete and/or cooperate to achieve certain goals, which may or may not be defined by the game. In many cases, these games can be played on multiple platforms. Most of these games target elementary-age children and adolescents. For example, Marvel Super Hero Squad Online™, is appropriate for elementary age children, while the extremely popular World of Warcraft™ and Guild Wars 2™ are more appropriate for adolescents and beyond. Although many MMOs are console or PC-based, there are increasing numbers of games that are playable on mobile devices and smartphones, one example being the very popular Clash and Clans™.

Digital games are a relatively recent innovation, and as such, comparisons can only be made to early forms of these games from a few decades ago. Digital games have very quickly evolved in terms of realism and complexity, and these rapid changes have made it difficult to assess the impact that these games will have, especially on brain development.

Representation Modes and Affordances of Digital Games

There is wide variation in the representation modes of digital games, especially in regard to the enactive mode. Also the affordances vary widely depending on the type of game and intentions of the game developer.

Representation Modes

The representation modes of digital games are very dependent on the game. Generally, nearly all digital games have significant emphasis on the *iconic* and *symbolic* modes. This is understandable given that these games must convey their message in an entertaining manner. In essence, digital games rely on the *iconic* and the *symbolic* to tell their stories. The *enactive* mode is the most controversial, because these games clearly require and thus promote a more sedentary type of play. One counterexample is the Wii system. Some Wii games, such as Wii Sports, require active participation by the player in terms of physical movements. Although the Wii system is high in terms of the enactive mode, in general digital games are extremely low on this dimension and this is becoming a major concern for those interested in the physical and natural-world development of children.

Affordances

The transparency, challenge, and accessibility of digital games also may vary greatly depending on the game and on the perspective taken by the designers.

For example, interaction with a digital game is via a device and/or a controller, and that controlling method can have high transparency if it is designed to convey its use. On the other hand, if the perspective is less about the control and more about the game itself, then there is great variability in transparency because the game developer would determine the method of control. In many cases, both the controlling medium and the game mechanics are intuitive and signal their use to the player. In general, transparency could be classified as high because these games depend heavily on players being able to grasp the interaction quickly, thus increasing the entertainment value of the games. Challenge, similar to transparency, is dependent on perspective. For the most part, the player only has a set amount of buttons with which to interact in the game. Thus, the player is simply pressing the same buttons or controller repeatedly, although the effects may result in contextual changes. Challenge is therefore minimal from the perspective of game control. From the perspective of the games themselves, challenge can be extremely varied. Challenge ranges from low for games where the player performs the same tasks repeatedly to high for games that are more open-ended and encourage exploration. Accessibility is also a major issue in digital games because of the current emphasis on "social" and "connected." However, similar to technology-augmented toys, group play with digital games can easily resemble individual play, but within a shared space. In many instances, children simply bring their own devices and literally sit beside their peers in silence, although they may be playing the same multiplayer game competitively or cooperatively. In this case, although players are connected via the electronic network, accessibility is low due to minimum personal interaction. They are playing the game and their peers happen to be playing as well. By the same token, some games are designed to have high transparency and accessibility. For example, the Nintendo Wii system was designed to accommodate group play in a literal and physical sense. For most of the Wii games, players must communicate, negotiate, share, and interact in a very literal manner, and this type of group play has both high transparency and accessibility.

Online Play Environments

The online play environment is a unique and very recent aspect of the virtual context. Unlike digital games, there is no winning, no points to obtain, and no proverbial "gold" to acquire. The online play environment simply describes the social communities that exist in the virtual online world. These communities for the most part mirror conventional communities, and online communities are based on themes that mostly concern adults. There are some differences that may have implications especially for the development of children because there are increasing numbers of communities designed for younger members of society. For example, some communities created by the Public Broadcasting Service (PBS) and National Geographic target infants, toddler, and preschoolers. PBS Kids features games and other activities based on PBS characters such as Clifford and Curious

George. Similarly, National Geographic Little Kids offers a variety of activities in an effort to both entertain and teach. Elementary-age children have many choices in terms of online play environments. Communities such as Barbie's My World and the Lego community are based on specific toys, but others such as Miss O & Friends, an online community specifically for young girls, are more general in nature. For adolescents, online play environments are currently a large portion of their activities and identities, and a significant portion of time is spent using social networking services (SNS). Popular options such as Reddit, an SNS where users vote on content; Twitter, an SNS that lets users send short (140 characters or less) messages or "tweets"; and Facebook, an SNS that connects individuals and facilitates relationships, are environments where adolescents can "hang out."

Representation Modes and Affordances of Online Play Environments

The majority of online play environments do not have enactive mode components, but they use iconic and symbolic modes extensively. They vary on these two dimensions, depending on the purposes or environments.

Representation Modes

Generally, online play environments are rich in iconic and symbolic representations, but very low in terms of the enactive mode. Although there are overall differences in iconic and symbolic representations, the extreme outlier is the enactive mode because most interaction in online play environments require little more than clicking a mouse or tapping a touchscreen. It is true that there may be cognitive benefits from the prevalence of iconic and symbolic representations, but the absence of enactive representations may be detrimental especially to younger children. The three representation modes are not balanced in the online play environment, and this may have implications for cognitive development. Interestingly, recent advances in virtual reality technology may be able to address the issue of lack of enactive representation in online play environments. Systems like the Oculus Rift, PrioVR, STEM, and Control VR will allow users to be fully immersed in the digital environment. These systems may eventually change how interaction occurs in online play environments, and allow for significant enactive representation. Consequently, virtual reality systems may restore some balance in terms of representation modes.

Affordances

Similar to digital games, the transparency, challenge, and accessibility of online play environments may vary greatly depending on the environment. In most cases, however, these environments are asynchronous—as opposed to the online digital games, which are mostly, but not exclusively, synchronous. Transparency is mostly high in online play environments, as users are able to quickly master the mechanisms required for interaction. This is evident in the rise of social network services, where users are able to quickly master the processes required for communication and interaction. Challenges range from low to high depending on the environment. In some sense, individuals are performing the same tasks repetitively, for example, updating one's Facebook status. From a different perspective, however, it can be argued that the act of updating is not limited to simply inputting text or images, but there is significant cognitive processing involved in constructing the post. In this perspective, challenge is high, because the situations and circumstances are dynamic within the online play environment. Another perspective on challenge centers on what individuals actually do in online play environments. Although participating in the environment may involve significant cognitive processing, participation is not a requirement. In most cases, individuals spent more time observing or "lurking" than they do contributing (Pempek et al. 2009). Challenge would thus be low because in reality, the tasks are mainly repetitive. While transparency and challenge may be low, accessibility is very high in online play environments. By design, these environments are social and they connect individuals in a variety of ways. Connections in this environment are virtual, and there is a real limitation in terms of individuals not being able to share the same physical space. In a sense, online play environments allow humans to socialize with many friends, while sitting alone in their rooms. Similar to digital games, the question of being social and connected "all by yourself" remains valid; thus, viewed from this perspective, accessibility appears to be low. Increasingly, however, online play environments are being viewed as legitimate communities with real effects (Hampton et al. 2011). The socializing and connections are real, even if the physical space is not shared. Within this perspective, accessibility is very high.

Potential Developmental Effects of Changing Representation Modes and Affordances in Play

Certainly there are questions as to whether social and emotional development may be affected by the change from face-to-face embodied human play interactions to ones represented by virtual iconic and symbolic interactions. For example, the ability to interpret facial expressions and meanings from language tones, which is enhanced during pretend play and social game play may not be promoted during virtual play interactions. Similarly, moral reasoning and cognitive capabilities such as attention, perspective-taking, and executive functioning may not be drawn upon or may be accessed differently during virtual play interactions. Research is needed in order to understand potential problems or perhaps advantages of such play in regard to the development of these valuable human characteristics.

FIGURE 3.1 We had fun building things!

FIGURE 3.2 See the tower grow tall!

FIGURE 3.3 The airplane is almost finished.

FIGURE 3.4 Can I match the shapes?

Activities and Questions for Discussion

1. Present a technology-augmented toy to an infant or toddler and demonstrate two of the technology-augmented actions once. Observe the subsequent actions of the child and list them in the order of their occurrence. Then determine the transparency level, challenge, and accessibility of this toy. Speculate on the types of learning that the toy provides and what types of learning it does not provide.

2. Observe an elementary-age child as she or he plays a digital game. Try to interrupt the child by asking her or him to perform a task or take a walk, and then note the results. Consider video recording the child as she or he plays and as you try to interrupt her or him. Play the recording back to child and discuss what the recording suggests and the implications.

3. Interview two adolescents and find out their favorite online play environments. Try to get a sense of how much time they spend and what exactly they do in this environment. Finally, find out how the adolescents perceive their relationships with others online, that is, how much of a "friend" are their online friends.

References

Bergen, D. (2001). Technology in the classroom: Learning in the robotic world: Active or reactive? *Childhood Education, 78*(1), 249–250.

Hampton, K., Goulet, L.S., Rainie, L., & Purcell, K. (2011). Social networking sites and our lives. Available at: http://www.academia.edu/download/30472786/Social_networking_sites_and_our_lives_2011.pdf

Pempek, T.A., Yermolayeva, Y.A., & Calvert, S.L. (2009). College students' social networking experiences on Facebook. *Journal of Applied Developmental Psychology, 30*(3), 227–238.

4

COMPARING DEVELOPMENTAL INFLUENCES OF TECHNOLOGY-AUGMENTED PLAY

Researchers', Parents', and Children's Perspectives

Brad is a rather quiet child who has had some difficulty making friends since his move to a new middle school. Recently he has joined a gaming group online that he seems to be enjoying and he has found that his interactions with the players, who are from many parts of the world, are very satisfying. His dad is not opposed to his enjoyment of such games as long as he gets his schoolwork done and his grades are good. However, he is somewhat concerned that Brad is spending more and more of his time online with the gaming group and is not making much of an effort to make new friends at the middle school. His dad has been urging him to find a club at school that he also would enjoy and he wants him to attend the football games but Brad says he doesn't have anyone to go with to those games and there isn't any good club to join. He also does not want his dad to go with him to the football games. He says, "I have my friends online."

Although it is very likely that technology-augmented play experiences will interact with play development, brain maturation, cognitive growth, and social development somewhat differently than experiences of play with more traditional toys and games and that these differences may result in disparate outcomes, at the present time there are only a few studies that have explored developmental dimensions and none of these studies as yet have provided longitudinal data related to effects of such play. However, a number of studies conducted by the authors and their colleagues and students can give insights into the potential short-term outcomes of technology-augmented play. Parents and children also have opinions about what the current and long-term developmental effects of play with technology-augmented play materials might be and how best to balance these various types of play. These opinions range from ones that see both traditional and technology-augmented play as having beneficial long-term effects to ones that see some problematic long-term outcomes of technology-augmented play. A sample of these opinions is provided in this chapter.

Research Studies on Short-Term Effects of Technology-Augmented Toy Play

Bergen and her colleagues and students have conducted a number of studies investigating the short-term effects of introducing young children to a variety of technology-augmented play materials. The first experimenntal study investigated the effects of children's play with "talking" and "non-talking" replica figures (Bergen, 2004, 2007), the second compared effects of a "talking" book to experience with traditional books (Strigens, Vondrachek, & Wilson, 2006), and the third examined parent and infant responses to a technology-augmented toy designed to encourage child action competencies and language growth (Bergen, Hutchinson, Nolan, & Weber, 2010).

The *first study* compared children's play with Rescue Hero™ figures with backpacks that enabled them to say commands and warnings with the same figures that did not have these technological features. It involved 64 preschool children (32 M; 32 F) from Head Start and other preschool programs who played on two occasions. About 30% of the children were African American, with the rest being Caucasian. A random assignment on three variables was used: talking/ non-talking toys, alone/peer play, Rescue Hero video/non-video viewing. Parents also completed a questionnaire about their child's play with replica figures before the experimental study was conducted. About one-fourth of the parents reported that their children had Rescue Hero figures, about one-half indicated their children had other "action figures," and almost three-fourths indicated that their children played with other replica figures such as dolls or animals. About one-half of the children had watched Rescue Hero videos or TV presentations. All children were videotaped at play with three Rescue Hero figures (male police officer, male firefighter, female firefighter) in a room at their preschools on two occasions about 3 weeks apart. The children also had a small set of wooden table blocks that could be used in the play. The questions of interest were whether there would be differences in children's play themes and language when playing with "talking" or "non-talking" figures and differences in themes or language when playing with a peer or playing alone. Also, whether there would be effects on the play themes of observing a video of Rescue Heroes was a question of interest.

Results of the study indicated that in the first session both the paired and the alone children primarily exhibited exploratory actions such as inspecting and using implements (with non-talking figures), and pushing talk buttons, removing, and replacing backpacks (with talking figures). They also engaged in elaborated actions such as making the toys fly, walk, and sit. However, pretend themes were more prominent in the second session. Many of the themes incorporated the features of the toys although some children made much more elaborated themes and some overrode the message the talking toys gave by using familiar themes from their experiences. For example, after putting out the fire (a direction given by the talking toy) one pair of children had the figures go home to sleep and made pillows of the blocks. Another pair removed the backpacks and had the female figure make dinner for "dad" and "brother." A child alone made a "trampoline" from the blocks and had all three figures jumping on that. Overall, however, there was a significant difference between the talking and non-talking groups on the types of actions in which they engaged, with the talking toys eliciting more Rescue Hero theme play. Watching the Rescue Hero videotape before the second session did result in clearer themes of this type in the second session pretense.

There were also significant differences between the peer and alone play patterns, with the peer play having more pretend themes, more Rescue Hero themes, and more elaborated construction using the blocks as part of the pretense. Children with Rescue Hero at home had more Rescue Hero themes. There were few gender differences, although the girls were especially in command of the female firefighter in most of the peer groups. Language observed included making the toys talk (in both conditions), describing attributes of the toys, and labeling toy actions and block structures. Children playing alone had a high proportion of egocentric speech while peer players had higher collaborative, control, oblige, and pragmatic statements and their pretense was more elaborate.

The presence of a peer resulted in longer times in play, more varied actions, more pretend themes, more labeling, and more describing the toys and toy actions. The best "enhancement" of the play appeared to be the presence of another child! Those children who had Rescue Hero toys at home did use more typical Rescue Hero themes. Because this was a short-term study it is impossible to say whether daily immersion in the themes through videos, toys, and access to such play would not have made the themes of play become less diverse and more tied to the messages the toys were sending.

In regard to the affordances of the toys, the transparency of both sets was low initially for most children so there was a high level of exploratory behavior before play occurred. The challenge of the talking toys was greater initially because the procedures for making the toy talk had to be learned. Some children met that challenge by disabling the talking capability and returning to familiar play themes. The presence of a peer greatly enhanced the accessibility of the toy and being able to talk about the toys and their features enabled the peer play to be more elaborated than the alone play. Many of the children used the cognitive schema they had from past play experiences, although there was some evidence that schema change also occurred.

The *second study*, conducted by three of Bergen's students, was designed to examine the effects of the PowerTouch™ "talking book" toy on children's language and reading progress. There were 60 Head Start children (20% first language Spanish) in the study, which was conducted over 3 months. The children were randomly assigned to either the talking or non-talking book condition. The graduate students visited the sites weekly and observed each child playing alone with either the talking book or with a set of other books. The questions of interest were whether the talking book would have a positive effect on print awareness, letter knowledge, and construction of meaning from print, and whether there would be a differential effect on boys and girls or on children whose native language was Spanish. Results did not support more positive reading and language effects from the talking book, however. There was no difference in emerging literacy skills between the two groups or for the Spanish-speaking children. The major differences found was in the larger amount of exploratory behavior rather than engagement with literacy aspects in the talking toy condition and the higher total engagement time spent with the talking toy condition compared to the book condition. Girls did have higher emergent literacy skills in both conditions. Recently, another study (Wooldridge & Shapka, 2012) has reported that parent and toddler engagement in a "talking book" resulted in a lower quality of parent/child interaction than in the typical book reading condition. There was more exploratory action rather than literacy engagement. It may be that in both cases, the novelty of the technology-augmented book superseded the literacy purposes of the book. Whether exposure to the talking book over a longer and more intense period of time would result in better enhancement of literacy is presently unknown.

In regard to affordances, the transparency issue was relevant in this study because the technology-augmented book had so many features to explore that its use at a deeper literacy level was not established. The challenge of just learning all of the features of the talking book was very high and since the children were exploring on their own without either another child or adult to engage them in greater accessibility, this aspect was not facilitated. Long-term exposure to such talking books with the presence of adult or competent peer engagement may result in higher levels of learning so longitudinal study of this type of toy that includes a social support component is needed.

The *third study*, done in collaboration with colleagues from the Department of Speech and Hearing, investigated whether the Laugh and Learn™ infant toy, which was specifically designed to encourage infant learning of motor skills and language growth, was effective in doing so. It involved 52 infants between the ages of 7 months and 28 months, half of whom were randomly assigned to biweekly parent/child play with the toy and half of whom served as control. Both groups received a toy at the end of the study. The sessions consisted of 5 minutes of infant play with the toy while the parent watched in the same room and then 20 minutes of parent/child play. Directions to parents were merely that they should play with the toy with their child. The sessions were videotaped and coded for play and language interactions. Instances of child laughter were also coded. A home instrument that the parent completed before the sessions started and after three sessions was administered and parents in both groups participated in a telephone interview 1 year later. Communicative interactions of child and parent during the first and last sessions were transcribed and coded, using the Systematic Analysis of Language Transcripts (SALT), and the Rossetti instrument describing child language was also completed at pre- and post-session time periods.

The affordance features of the toy that significantly facilitated parent/child communication were the mailbox, blocks, and balls. The typical pattern of play was parent initiation and child response; child response was significantly correlated with parent initiations, thus fostering joint attention. Social games initiated by the parents such as "peek-a-boo" using the door or window elicited the strongest laughter from the children. Over 30% of the time was spent in exploration of the toy, with about 40% being practice play with its features (putting balls down the spout, activating the radio, opening and shutting the door). Social games accounted for over 20% of the time but pretend play was almost nonexistent (only 1%).

In regard to the parent survey of increases in home motor skills, parents reported that after the third session, there were significant changes in child home activation of light switches, doorbells, keys, opening and shutting toy mailboxes, and turning on the radio. In the 1-year survey, parents reported that the door, radio, and mailbox were still the most independent play actions of their children. Many reported that the child continued to play with the toy after 1 year.

Language analysis showed that during the experimental sessions parents primarily used verbalizations, directives, demonstrations, and focusing attempts related to toy features. Parents' Mean Length of Utterance for both word and morpheme use significantly increased from first to last session and child utterances also increased. For language-delayed children, parents were more likely to use language that required an action response rather than a language response. The comparison of the experimental and control groups on child language growth did not show a significant difference between these groups of children. That is, the children who did not participate in the study had similar language growth as did the children who did participate. Interestingly, another recent study of infant language learning that involved infants watching a DVD that highlighted words related to household objects (Robb, Richert, & Wartella, 2009) did not find increased growth in language from watching the video many times. In that study, the significant predictor of vocabulary growth was the amount of time that the adults read to the infants.

The affordances of the Laugh and Learn toy were similar initially to those in the other two studies. That is, transparency of the features of the toy was initially low for both parent and child so there was a high level of exploratory behavior. Because the toy had so many technology-augmented features there were many aspects to explore even in the following sessions, which may be why so little pretense was ever observed. The challenge of operating the features of the toy was initially great and primarily involved motor play and social games rather than pretense. Many aspects of the toy's accessibility were enhanced by parent involvement and parental encouragement was needed for many children to become engaged in play with the toy. An initial goal of the manufacturers was to improve infant's cognitive schema related to the instrumental tasks of door opening, light switching, and other home tasks and the toy did seem to facilitate that goal.

Research Studies of Elementary-Age Children's Videogame Play

Two pilot studies of the ERP wave patterns of children ages 7–11 as they played a computer game that consisted of two types of prompts have also been conducted (Bergen, Chou, Wilks, Lyman & Thomas, 2013; Schroer, Bergen, Thomas, & Zhang, 2015). One prompt required the child to press the key that corresponded to the correct color name for sets of geometric shapes that were icons of 'alien creatures' (*color* identification) while the other prompt asked the child to select between two imaginary (*choice* options), such as *what food would the creature like?*, that did not involve a right/wrong comparison. The overall hypothesis was that the nature of the child interactions with video games that have varied affordances may affect brain activation in different ways. That is, a game that involves simple choices between right/wrong stimuli may activate brain areas that are focused on evaluating correct responses while other areas might be activated in a game that involved creative choices between equally appropriate answers.

The *first study*, conducted with children primarily from high socioeconomic backgrounds (mean age 107 months), found differences in the mean amplitude of the P300 wave patterns in areas of the brain involved in stimulus evaluation, with the choice condition showing greater wave amplitude than the color identification condition at Pz (parietal) and the color condition showed greater wave amplitude at Cz and Fz (central and frontal). Reduction in the P300 amplitude occurs when it is necessary to inhibit some aspects of a task to focus on a task relevant dimension (for a review, see Polich, 2013). The P300 amplitude typically increases with novelty, importance, or other characteristics that encourage memory encoding processes. That the choice trials yielded greater P300s than the correct/incorrect color identification task fits with this pattern.

In contrast, because "working" memory systems have greater activation for tasks that involve holding more information in the system or require inhibiting irrelevant information, the cognitive "load" is greater and the P300 wave amplitude is smaller. If the stimulus is novel, important, or otherwise interesting, P300 increases. For the correct/incorrect questions, the children had to focus on that dimension and inhibit others, and that reduced the P300 amplitude. On the choice tasks, the P300 wave increased because the task was more novel, interesting, or important. Analysis of the N200 wave, which is involved in object recognition tasks, showed that the color identification condition resulted in higher amplitudes of wave responses at Pz, but lower amplitude at Fz. There were no differences between boys and girls on these tasks.

The *second study* was conducted with children from a wider range of socioeconomic backgrounds (mean age 119 months), in order to examine whether the differences found in the first study also would be found across socioeconomic groups. In this study, the choice condition again showed significantly higher P300 and P100 mean amplitudes at Pz. The choice condition also elicited a greater P300 amplitude than the color condition at Cz and a slightly larger N200 mean amplitude for the color condition at Cz, but not at Fz. Both studies showed that children demonstrated a greater positive amplitude of N200 and P300 in the choice condition at Pz and the replication confirmed that similar results for the P300 wave were found across all three electrode points and all four conditions. The second study also found a significant difference in P300 at Pz between the color and choice conditions.

There was a significant interaction effect found in the second study, which may be due to the age levels of the children. An independent samples t-test revealed statistically significant differences at two electrodes involving mixed choice condition for the younger and older halves of the group. On average younger students exhibited a more positive inflected mean amplitude (M= 3.23, SE = 1.50) than older students (M = −3.26, SE = 1.09) at Fz during the mixed choice condition ($t(13)$= 3.60, p < .005). Conversely, on average older students exhibited a more positive inflected mean amplitude (M = 3.89, SE = 1.72) than younger students (M = −3.78, SE = 0.863) at Pz during the mixed choice condition ($t(13)$= −3.41, p < .01). This indicates that there was a stronger focus on attention at the frontal lobe site for younger children during the mixed conditions suggesting they needed to put more attention resources into the mixed task. Since the older children showed a more positive inflection in the parietal lobe this may indicate that older children instead put more mental resources into the decision-making process. Younger children may have had more cognitive load in the mixed choice condition and thus had problems set shifting.

The results of these studies support the hypothesis that different types of video game play that have varied affordances may activate brain waves differently. The children in both studies paid more effortful attention in the choice condition. The results confirmed the hypothesis that there would be a deeper stimulus evaluation and activation of memory traces in the parietal lobe during the choice condition (see Patel & Azzam, 2005) and that the N200 and P300 wave amplitudes would be larger in the color condition in the frontal lobe, which is consistent with findings by Lange et al. (1998). Although these studies confirm the hypotheses regarding possible differences in children's brain activation when they are playing video games with different affordances that call on varied skills, further study is needed to probe the meaning of these differences.

Accompanying the second of these studies was a survey of the parents and children regarding the children's video game play (Zhang, 2015) and significant differences were found between how parents and children viewed video game play. Parents preferred educational video games more than children did and they indicated that there were games they did not like to have their children play. Also, parents were more in agreement with putting time limits on videogame play than children were and they were more likely to say that children spent too much time playing videogames. The only statement that children scored higher than parents was on their agreement that they liked to play games that were difficult. Younger children (6–8) agreed more than older children (9–12) did that there were some videogames that parents do not like their children to play. This may mean that parents monitor younger children's video game play more than they monitor older children's video game play. Parents indicated that children learned problem-solving skills, cooperation, critical thinking, and creativity from playing video games while children had more varied answers, including dancing, persistence, and academic learning. Only 35% of the parents knew all of the games their children played and 15% could not name any of the games their children listed. Minecraft was the most popular game mentioned, and other popular games were Clash of Clans™ and Jetpack Joyride™.

Parent and Child Interview Data on Play Experiences

Structured interviews recently were conducted with a convenience sample of parents and children to learn more about the current dynamics of child play. Parents and children were asked to describe favorite play at various age levels and to give their views about the influences of their play on learning and development.

Parent Interviews of Young Children's Experiences

The parents of the youngest group of children all gave many examples of their children's favorite play, some types that did not involve any technology-augmented toys and some that did include toys that made sounds, "talked," gave directions, played music, or included some other type of electronic-based action. The parent of a 1½-year-old child stated that her daughter's favorite non-tech play was with board books and baby dolls. She engages in brief pretend feeding with the dolls and enjoys opening the "flaps" in the books to see the pictures. However, even many of the books have electronic features such as playing music or making animal noises. This parent said that she thought the non-technology play was more creative and involved "a little pretend" such as feeding her doll. Examples parents gave of favorite non-tech or low-tech play materials of their 3- and 4-year-olds included play with wheeled vehicles (cars and trucks, an ambulance, a school bus, trains on wooden tracks), and play with small figures (e.g., Little People™, Transformers™, Power Rangers™) and their accompanying materials (e.g., playhouses, garages, farms). Many of these toys do have technology-augmented sounds or give directions but most of these parents indicated that the children did not just follow the directions but usually invented their own play themes. As one parent commented, "the play is independent of the toy themes; she is more likely to replay scenarios from her preschool." Another said her child had many favorites among the technology-augmented toys especially because he "likes to take them apart and put them together" but that he was "still attached to his stuffed Elmo™," a toy that does not make a noise. Another commented that her daughter preferred imaginative play and that she preferred her daughter "learn through her environment" because "play is her world."

Parents had many examples of technology-augmented play that their young children enjoyed. One parent indicated that when her child was 1½ he liked the Laugh and Learn™ toy because "he could crawl in and out of the gate, ring the doorbell, work the light switch, press the radio button, and spin the sun and moon" and she thought that he had learned skills that transferred to the real world and helped him understand cause-and-effect relationships. The toddler girl also plays with technology-augmented toys such as the Leapfrog Touch Magic Bus™ that recites the alphabet and when the driver is pushed in his seat, lights flash and he says phrases. She has a Playskool Pink Elephant™ that makes sounds when its trunk is pulled and a Fisher Price Laugh and Learn Laptop™ that says alphabet letters and numbers. When she was even younger she liked the Baby Einstein Activity Center™. Her mother thinks that her attention span is longer with the technology-augmented toys and that "they are wonderful for cause and effect." Since her daughter loves music, many of the toys can sing repeatedly and although "that's not quite as good as a parent singing, I get tired of singing the same songs." Although her daughter is very interested in her parent's iPhone this parent says that she does not let her hold it unless it is "locked." Another parent indicated that her 2½-year-old child likes to watch "wheels on the bus" and other animated versions on YouTube™ and he also watches

Curious George and Sesame Street on TV. He only has access to the iPad when "it is a break for us!" She said, "I am not a big video game person and think we spend too much time on electronic devices." In contrast, another parent said that she allows her child to have a "movie night" on TV and her child is allowed to use iPad apps that are learning games. She thinks the game apps help her learn letters, numbers, and basic reading skills. The idea that apps are good for teaching young children the alphabet and numbers is a view that was common to most of the parents, but they also expressed concerns and limited their children's time on such devices. For example, one said, "If allowed, he would do it for hours and hours so that's why I limit time. I prefer he go outdoors and play and he does love to be outside." Another said, "The cause/effect is too black and white on the iPad."

The parents all agreed that their play as children differed greatly from the play of their own children. Most mentioned outside play as prominent in their childhood and they remembered playing various ball games and board games and "using imagination" in their own play. One said that she would play "for hours" with her dolls and "I talked for them." She also played ball games with her brother. In regard to digital game play on devices such as iPads and computer game play, the parents of these young children have mixed feelings. Although most did not have major concerns about their children's technology-augmented play and, as one parent said, "What I pick for her is developmentally appropriate and designed well without hazards," they do not want their children to "be too dependent on technology" because it is important to "play with other kids" and in such play their "imagination leads them." They also agreed that technology knowledge is a part of the present environment and will give them "a heads up on some computing skills, help them play independently, and hold their attention." As one parent concluded about her child's technology-augmented play, "At least he will be familiar with what he will do for the rest of his life."

Parent Interviews of Elementary-Age Children's Play Experiences

Parents of the children in this age bracket acknowledged that their children had a range of technology play options although they still enjoyed play with other types of toys that they had played with at younger ages. For example, one parent listed blocks, trucks, Lego constructions, pretense with Star Wars™ figures, board games, and camping outdoors as other play her son has enjoyed. Two other parents also mentioned Legos and small action figures as continuing to be favorite play materials, and one said "although the Legos are themed, he makes other things with them." Another agreed that in her child's play with Legos he "creates stories and his own scenes with figures; he doesn't stay with themes." She thinks he is gaining manual dexterity and imagination from this play. A parent who said her son "still likes pretending with tractors and trucks sometimes" stated that although some of these have batteries, "he preferred ones that he could control." Early play mentioned by one of the parents of a girl included stuffed animals, musical toys, a pretend house with a door and doorbell that could be activated, and outside play with chalk and finger paint. Another parent of two girls named board books, baby dolls, pretend shopping cart and dress-up clothes as favorites. She said, "Their play time seemed to be all the time." At elementary age, this parent stated that American Girl™ dolls, Build a Bear™, and electronic tablets like iPads were favorite playthings. Other non-tech activities parents mentioned that their children are engaged in during play were reading and making origami creatures and designs.

The favorite technology-augmented play mentioned by most of these parents either involved the XBox™, the iPad, or the iPhone. The parents said the Xbox type games are sometimes played alone but often include siblings or friends, and they agreed that children learn "social interactions" during this play. However, they also expressed the view that "XBox is not creative." One parent said that from the iPad and iPhone play her son was gaining eye-hand coordination and spatial reasoning, although most of the games are "predefined" so they also are not increasing his imagination. She suggested that Minecraft is more creative than most of the other technology-augmented play options. Another parent reported that Minecraft is the primary type of virtual play she permits for her child. He also plays Clash of Clans and RISK™ but she has to restrict his time on Minecraft to about 1–2 hours a day because he would "play all day." If he does not do other required activities well, then she restricts the Minecraft time. She believes many of the online games are "too violent" and this type of play "can't be monitored as well" as other types of activities. Another parent had similar views, saying, "I had to put a limit on it; it could have been 5 hours so we 'put the hammer down' and he can play no more than 3 hours." One dad agreed that Minecraft and Clash of Clans were favorites of his son and said, "I am not concerned as we have a good balance, although my wife is more concerned than I am." He notes, however, that "electronic devices don't allow imagination, although sometimes they (the children) can get an idea and then make their own play." He thinks his children "know their own limit." This parental difference of opinion also was expressed by another parent who said she and her husband had different views, with the wife "setting more limits."

The parent of one of the girls reported that about half of her child's play time was with technology-augmented toys and that she spent about 2–3 hours in such play after school. She spends time on PBSKids.org website with games based on the animated TV program "Wild Kratts," in which she can "learn about animals." The other parent of girls estimated they spent about an hour after school in technology-augmented play although the older girl is now watching more TV. The types of play these girls engage in include Minecraft, Wipeout™,

Subway Surfer™, and girlsgogames.com. One parent concluded, "They have a good sense for the different uses of a computer or table, including playing games and finding information, but they do not have a good sense for the reliability of that information." The other said, "They learn about different topics not covered in school."

The types of play that parents engaged in as children are somewhat different from the present play of their children. One parent indicated that he was involved in sports, building models, climbing trees, and walking in the woods. Another lived on a farm and mainly played outside, which involved "exploring by the creek," "riding bikes," and "swinging on a swing set." Another said, "I played with others; we put on shows and didn't rely on toys." None of them reported having much engagement in technology-augmented play. However, as one parent said, "There are different toys and devices but the play is pretty much the same—games, pretending, making, and creating. The one difference is that it is much easier for a child to play a game today without needing another person and they don't need to cooperate as much to figure out something to play that multiple people will enjoy." Another agreed that today's children have "easier access to a wider variety of materials" and "The world is a little bigger because of this internet."

In regard to concerns about technology-augmented play, a number of parents had "yes and no" answers. One said, "It's something we have to limit and also keep talking with them about good behavior and good balance with using mobile devices . . . and we sometimes have to force the kids to turn off the TV and go outside, but that was pretty much the same as when I was a kid." Perhaps that is why most of these parents have some concerns about its long-term effects. One stated a concern that "Not all parents monitor as we do" and stated that children still need physical activity, face-to-face interactions, and imagination. Another said that "it is a limitation in many ways (because) they believe everything should be at their fingertips and they are quick to jump on the first information they find without thinking too hard about it. They haven't learned how to do things without technology so they rarely appreciate what it can do." A positive feature expressed by one parent was that children now may be "more willing to think outside of the box and be more willing to explore." A third parent commented, "I am concerned with overexposure but I know this is what the future holds. I think parents who don't let their children have such play will have their kids at a disadvantage."

Parent Interviews of Adolescents' Play Experiences

The views of parents of adolescents also covered a wide range. One parent reported that her son's favorite early playthings were wooden blocks, small figures, Thomas™ trains, and little cars (Matchbox™ Hot Wheels™) and in elementary age these favorites were elaborated into "small worlds" with long stories made up for the characters that went on for days and even resulted in video stories about them. Drawing was always a favorite activity also. His technology-augmented play did not really start until he was in about third grade, with a handheld Nintendo DS™, although he used a LeapPad™ at kindergarten age to learn state capitals and bone names, and at later ages played with Animal Crossing™ and Sim City™. This parent estimated that at elementary age her son spent about 30% of his play time on technology-augmented devices, but his major non-technology play continued to be drawing and designing books of story plots so creativity was a prominent learning result. She says, "I'm not sure what he learned from Nintendo DS, but probably learned some critical thinking, puzzle strategies to solve problems and get to a goal." With the other two games, he developed a "fantasy of real life" and also these "sparked his interests in maps." This parent also described her daughter's play (sister of the boy) and indicated her early play was with stuffed animals, dolls (American Girls™), wooden blocks, and horse figures, as well as board games. The "small worlds" and game play was usually with her brother. Very little of her play was with technology-augmented play materials even in elementary school, although she did have a LeapPad and Nintendo DS and sometimes played with Sims on the computer. The mother estimated that her daughter spent less than 5% of her time in technology-related play. Building with blocks enhanced her fine motor skills and pretending and making up stories with her brother enhanced her creativity. The only learning from technology that the parent recalled was the reading and geography skills learned on the iPad. Another parent who did not encourage technology-augmented play until her son was about 12 indicated that when he was younger his play involved reading books, listening to cassette tapes, doing puzzles, and playing board games and card games with family members. She states, "I think he learned pre-reading skills and an early love of books from these kinds of play." He now plays games online but still has a wide range of other interests. The play one of these parents engaged in as a child "was more interactive with her siblings." They engaged in creative pretense, singing, and making up plays. She said they also played board games, often with other family members. The other parent said her play was more "gender stereotyped" and also more "violent."

In regard to the pros and cons of technology-augmented play, one parent expressed a concern about such play being "addictive, too fast moving sometimes, and it can make imagination less necessary. Also, it can be violent and have sexual content if a parent is not very careful to monitor." The parent who did not allow early access to technology-augmented play had strong views about the issue of advantages and disadvantages to such play. She stated,

"I think technology often replaces self-discipline and human contact. Children don't have to wait or confront difficult situations because technology keeps them busy." She also thinks some parents use it as "an easy babysitter." On the other hand, she noted that more experience with technology play might have given her son "a leg up" with friends who did have the latest technology-augmented toys. Another parent said that computer skills and other types of technology skills were gained from these devices. However, she also said she "can't decide if technology games are positive since the problem is they can be so addicting and don't promote patience." A parent of adolescents who use social media said parents have to help their children know how to engage in ways that don't result in destroying relationships and self-confidence. She said, "They don't know how to navigate and interpret the social comments that can be painful or even bullying." In the online world, "you follow not just friends but acquaintances and engage with people you have limited knowledge of" and adolescents will often "say something to elevate status or say things they shouldn't be saying. There is a lot of hurt and kids don't have filters to properly keep from saying and interpreting hurtful things." She thinks parents "have to engage with your children's friends' parents because online can get out of control."

Child and Adolescent Interviews on Play Experiences

Four elementary-age children and four adolescents were interviewed regarding their views on questions that were similar to the ones the adults answered.

Child Interviews of Their Play Experiences

The elementary-age boy who answered the questions said that when he was younger he liked building with blocks, playing with dinosaurs, and playing board games like Candyland™ but that now he liked to play Minecraft on the computer and on the iPad. He thinks he plays about two hours a day and says, "If I play too much I get sick of the game and get crabby." He thinks Minecraft is creative because you can "make different designs," but he doesn't spend too much time because "My mom won't let me." However, what he likes about it is that you can "make the computer build a world." On the iPad, he plays math games like Sumdog™ and he watches *Frego Rocks* on TV. He really likes reading books, though, like the *Hunger Games* and the *Edge Chronicles*. The 6-year-old girl said that playing Barbies and baby dolls, slinkees, letter magnets, and drawing were what she liked best when she was younger and her favorite play now continues to be Barbies but is also "iPad, trampoline, and crafts." She thinks she now spends about 45 minutes a day with video games or online experiences. Her favorite non-technology activity now is drawing and her favorite tech game is iPad Cooking game because, "You can bake anything that you want to, so I learn how to cook" (the game describes ingredients and child chooses and mixes together). She thinks her parents "probably played with wooden toys" and "TV wasn't in color." However, "we both had baby dolls." In regard to whether too much time is spent in such play, she says, "Yes–maybe. Kids want to play with tablets a lot and forget to turn it off." As an adult she thinks she "will only play on it sometimes so your kids don't keep asking you to play on it."

One of the 9-year-old girls agreed that play with dress-up, Barbies, and baby dolls were favorites when she was younger but now her favorites are "tablet computer, trampoline, and crafts." She plays with technology-augmented devices about 45 minutes a day, "but I'm not counting TV, since that's not play." The reason she likes crafts is because "you learn to express your unique qualities in what you make." Her favorite present tech play is Wipeout 2™ on the tablet but "you don't learn anything with that; it is all entertainment." She also likes playing Minecraft, "where I learn to be creative." She says, "My parents didn't have technology. They had some similar toys that we have." She is concerned about too much technology-augmented play because, "Now that it is in houses, lots of kids will just sit down with a device and play with it and they can't stop because they are too sucked into the game." However, the advantage of technology is that, "We will know how the technology works and have comparisons on how much technology we have and how much future kids will have."

The other 9-year-old girl identified her favorite early plaything as a stuffed toy named "Ted" that was always with her, but she also liked painting and sidewalk chalk drawing. Now, although she still has "Ted" her favorite play is with dot-to-dot books, reading, and fashion drawing. She also likes online games and spends about 2 hours each day using the computer or tablet. Her favorite is a dress-up game on a site that has games for girls (http://www.girlsgogames.com). She thinks her drawing helps her to learn "how to use my imagination and my creativity" and her play with Ted "shows me I can be independent." Her favorite technology-augmented play involves games on PBSkids.org and she thinks Wild Kratts™, which teaches you about animals, and other games like that are what she enjoys most. She thinks she spends too much time in technology play because "either I do my homework or play online . . . mostly I play online." As far as advantages in this type of play, she thinks Wild Kratts may help "because I want to be a vet and they help me learn about animals."

Adolescent Interviews of Their Play Experiences

The 14-year-old boy described his early play as reading books, playing card games, and playing board games like Monopoly™, Rail Baron™, and Titan™ with his dad and brother. Now his favorite play involves doing magic, playing card games, and engaging at Scouts in the Rise of Mythos™. He spends about 2 hours a day playing online games and he especially likes playing Country Geography™, which involves people from other parts of the world such as Indonesia and Europe. He says the play involves, "multilayer interaction with people from obscure countries" as you try to "play to become as powerful as you can" by gaining money and power. He knows his dad's favorite kind of play was doing magic tricks and engaging in card games. He sees both the pros and cons of technology-augmented play and thinks some people who play 5 or 6 hours a day are "wasting time and not doing the things you should be doing." However, he also sees advantages in this play because you meet people online, gain more options for society and become knowledgeable about technology.

The 13-year-old girl who was interviewed said that playing with dolls, dress-up, and drawing all were favorite activities when she was younger. She also liked riding her bike and playing soccer. Now, however, her favorite play is texting on her phone. She sends messages and pictures and spends about 2 or 3 hours a day doing it, "although not all at the same time, just throughout the day." She uses Instagram™ the most and, in comparison to others, she thinks she uses the "average amount" although it is still probably "too much." She thinks it makes her friendships stronger. However, if she was not doing that she states, "I could have played other games and been going outside to play soccer." She stated that she is very comfortable with technology because, "our generation grew up with it" and she feels that they know more about how to use it. She concluded by saying "we will be ready for the future."

The older adolescent girl who was interviewed described her favorite play during second and third grade as imaginative play with the Polly Pocket™ small figures and the many small animal figures she had from play sets. She liked to play with friends and set up "pet shops" because "I love animals." With her friends she would make up stories. The only technology-augmented device she remembers playing with was Nintendo DS GameBoy™ where she played Animal Crossing™. She said in this game she also could make up stories. In response to the question of what her favorite play is in adolescence she remarked, "Honestly, there isn't much because I don't use apps games; I just use my iPhone and social media sites." She spends time doing this with friends. However, she notes that some of the time is "pointless" just finding out what other people are doing. Sometimes she browses sites because "I like to get ideas about what to do for crafts." One app that she does like is Pinterest™, an online site where you can plan to buy clothes and get recipes but you don't really buy anything. "You are just making your dream life," she said. The learning she thinks you get from such play is how to make decisions. "You are not really learning anything valuable but you are learning about yourself and what you like." She also likes to take pictures on her iPhone and edit them and share them. However, she thinks she spends only about 1 or 2 hours with any electronic media and that "face to face is better." She really isn't sure what advantages there might be in the future with technology but she does think that the exploring type of play that she engages in online "makes me more creative and able to think outside the box, rather than staying with the same thing."

The older adolescent boy described his early play as involving Bionicles™, Legos, toy cars, action figures, and building blocks. Now his favorite forms of play are playing and listening to music, playing video games, and doing recreational research on the computer. He says he only plays online games a few hours a week though. He is more interested in playing the guitar and he thinks he has learned finger coordination and precision as well as a better ear for music from this play. The video games like Minecraft, Uncharted™, Red Dead Redemption™, and Metal Gear Solid 3™ have taught him strategy (in some cases) and in the more-fast-paced games he has learned better eye-hand coordination. He thinks his play is similar to his dad's play when he was young, but although he thinks his dad would have liked to play video games, his dad did not have access to them. He shares his musical interests with his mother though. In regard to the time he spends with technology he stated, "I don't spend a huge amount of time playing video games but I do probably spend too much time on the computer because it is used not only for schoolwork but also for communication, recreational reading, recording music, and other things."

Drawing Conclusions from the Evidence

Most of the research studies on technology-augmented play described in this chapter are of a short-term nature so long-term social, emotional, moral, or cognitive effects of play with such technology-augmented play materials cannot be predicted. However, they do indicate that the technology-augmented toys used in play had some differential effects on the children's play experiences and perhaps on various developmental areas, at least in the short term. The views on the past and present play experiences expressed by children, adolescents, and parents give some insights into the potential ways that technology-augmented play may make changes in human brain, social, emotional, moral, and cognitive development.

One insight gained was that it appears that the technology-augmented play world of boys and girls are somewhat different, at least for the group of participants interviewed. Also, there are factors that serve to exert pressure towards either increasing or limiting technology-augmented play. The tension created by often opposing pressures is evident in a situation described by a father of two elementary-aged children:

The girls had spent the night before at a friend's house and had been watching TV for a while that morning. It was eventually time to turn the TV off and get the kids doing something more active. The kids, of course, wanted to keep watching TV and began to plead for time playing on iPads instead of watching TV. My wife said "no" to all devices and left the girls to sort out what they would do to occupy themselves. I had been having the girls help me with a few tasks, during which they started playing a game between themselves. They ended up trying to play poker like they had seen kids doing in a movie they had watched at the sleepover the night before. They had watched a movie in which there was a scene with two sisters playing poker. My girls didn't really know what poker was, but they came up with a version idea of poker was this: (1) there were cards involved, but they had little idea of how that part of the game worked, and (2) they would put something of value (one of their toys) in the middle of them and, at the end, one of them would take everything in the middle. Of course, this game ended in a minor argument between the girls because the youngest wanted her stuff back.

Children have a tendency to continually increase their engagement with technology-augmented play materials as they grow older, although the forms of play as well as the nature of the technology-augmented play materials continually change. There is also a notable pressure that results from parents' perception of the value of the forms of play that can serve to either increase or decrease the use of technology in play. Parents who value technology as essential to future endeavors may be more willing to accept or even promote technology-augmented play. By contrast, parents who are apprehensive about the loss or decrease in forms of play that do not involve technology may seek to limit technology-augmented play as a means of promoting more balance with other forms of play.

Whether such play experiences will make the next generations more competent and adaptable to future societal challenges is presently unknown. However, there will certainly be dynamic system interactions among the representational modes, affordances, and contexts of these play experiences and among the dynamic system elements that are present in play development, brain development, and technology innovation.

Activities and Questions for Discussion

1. Interview a parent of a young child and find out what types of technology-augmented play the parent reports. Compare these views to the views expressed by parents about such play that were discussed in this chapter.

FIGURE 4.1 See what I did on my iPad!

FIGURE 4.2 This is my favorite iPad game!

FIGURE 4.3 It takes skill to make the ball move.

FIGURE 4.4 Learning how to play this game takes all my attention.

2. Select an elementary-age child and ask about two types of technology-augmented play materials that he or she uses. Analyze the representation modes and affordances these play materials offer. Speculate as to the differences in experience and possible learning that would be gained from the two.

3. Spend 1 hour observing an adolescent as he or she plays an online game or interacts with social media. Describe the affordances of the game and the types of representation mode that the player exhibits during the play. Speculate as to the cognitive, social, and emotional learning aspects that the game promotes.

References

Bergen, D. (2004). Preschool children's play with "talking" and "non-talking" Rescue Heroes: Effects of technology-enhanced figures on the types and themes of play. In J. Goldstein, D. Buckingham, & G. Brougere (Eds.), *Toys, games and media* (pp. 195–206). Mahwah, NJ: Erlbaum.

Bergen, D. (2007). Communicative actions and language narratives in preschoolers' play with "talking" and "non-talking" Rescue Heroes. In O. Jarrett & D. Sluss (Eds.), *Play investigations in the 21st century.* (*Play and Culture Series, Vol. 7,* J. Johnson, Series Ed., pp. 229–248). University Press of America.

Bergen, D., Chou, M., Wilks, T., Lyman, J., & Thomas, R. (2013, May). *Child responses to two video games differ by condition: An ERP study.* Poster presentation at Association for Psychological Science, Washington, DC.

Bergen, D., Hutchinson, K., Nolan, J., & Weber, D. (2010). Effects of infant-parent play with a technology-enhanced toy: Affordance related action and communicative interaction. *Journal of Research in Childhood Education, 24*(1), 1–17.

Lange, J.J., Wijers, A.A., Mulder, L.J., & Mulder, G. (1998). Color selection and location selection in ERPs: Differences, similarities and neural specificity. *Biological Psychology, 48*(2), 153–182.

Patel, S.H., & Azzam, P.N. (2005). Characterization of N200 and P300: Selected studies of the event-related potential. *International Journal of Medical Sciences, 2*(4), 147–154.

Polich, J. (2013). Neuropsychology of P300. In S. J. Luck & E. S. Kappenman (Eds.), *The Oxford handbook of event-related potential components.* New York: Oxford University Press.

Robb, M., Richert, R., & Wartella, E. (2009). Just a talking book? Word learning from watching baby videos. *British Journal of Developmental Psychology, 27*, 27–45.

Schroer, J., Bergen, D., Thomas, R., & Zhang, X. (2015*). Child ERP responses to two stimuli types in videogame simulations: Study 1 and 2 comparisons.* Presentation at the American Educational Research Association, Chicago.

Strigens, D., Vondrachek, S., & Wilson, J. (2006). *Comparisons of literacy effects of technology-enhanced and non-technology enhanced books.* Unpublished thesis. Miami University, Oxford, OH.

Wooldridge, M. B., & Shapka, J. (2012). Playing with technology: Mother–toddler interaction scores lower during play with electronic toys. *Journal of Applied Developmental Psychology, 33*(5), 211–218.

Zhang, X. (2015). *The perceptions of parents and children on video games and the effects of video games on children's brain development.* Unpublished masters project, Miami University, Oxford, OH.

5

PREDICTING THE BRAIN/PLAY/TECHNOLOGY INTERFACE IN FUTURE SOCIETY

Implications for Human Development

> Almost all of the favorite play activities of Will, age 8, who has been diagnosed with autism spectrum disorder, involve interactions with technology-augmented play materials. Will spends hours on the computer or iPad watching and responding to the actions of his "virtual friends." He describes these characters' actions and talks as though they are really present but has difficulty responding to "real-time" social interactions with other students or even with his parents and siblings. He did learn some social interaction behaviors in kindergarten by watching a video of a child demonstrating ways to play and language phrases to use during play with other children, but these play interactions did not expand into more nuanced social interactions and language as he grew older. He has learned academic skills and complex routines from a variety of computer-assisted programs, however, so his parents think he might become a computer programmer or work in some other technology field when he is older.

Predicting the future has always been an activity of interest to humans, and such predictions have been discussed by numerous writers. Depending on how the future is predicted from extrapolations of the authors' present society, some writers have described utopian (splendid) or dystopian (horrible) views of that future society, while others have combined elements of both. One of the first descriptions of a utopian civil society was described by Plato in his book *The Republic* (380 BC), but the word was first coined by Thomas More in his book entitled

Utopia (1516). Utopian views focus on the wonders and advantages that will be available in future years while dystopian literature points out how potentially negative characteristics of an existing society can become extreme and thus be harmful in the future. Often utopian literature includes some potentially grave choices that could lead to less desired outcomes or potential threats that might occur. For example, Swift's *Gulliver's Travels* (1726) described both good and not-so-good alternative societies. Movie series such as the Star Wars (1977–2015) group also juxtapose good and evil societal dimensions. The plots of the Star Trek television show invented by Gene Rodenberry (see Van Hise, 1992) often engaged the crew in evaluating positive or negative outcomes that might occur depending on the wisdom of human decisions. Video games like the Sims also allow players to create "ideal" worlds, but also face potential disasters that might destroy those worlds.

Well-known dystopian views have been expressed by Butler (*Erewhon*, 1921) and We (*Zamyatin*, 1921/1924) and more recently by Huxley (*Brave New World*, 1932), Orwell (*Nineteen Eighty-Four*, 1949), Bradbury (*Fahrenheit 451*, 1953), and Burgess (*A Clockwork Orange*, 1962). Some of these authors described societies in which technological and biological advances were used to create societies favoring special groups and subjugating other groups, while others predicted the loss of established knowledge sources (e.g., books) due to pervasive technological advances. In recent times there have been an increasing number of novels, movies, young adult fiction, and video games with dystopian themes. For example, the movies *Wall-E* and *Avatar* both describe earth's environmental ruins from destructive, technologically based decisions, and some current video games series, Fallout™ (a post-nuclear simulation) and Half-Life™ (science and aliens), also have dystopian themes.

On the 25th anniversary of a movie that envisioned a wonderful future world with many technological innovations (*Back to the Future II*, 1985), some futurists gave their reflections on what was and was not correctly predicted to be available in 2015. The movie envisioned time travel, flying cars, and many other technology marvels that still do not exist, but some of the many devices imagined are actually present in 2015 (Schonfeld, 2014). For example, the movie envisioned humans making video calls, using glasses similar to Google Glass, and having drones and hoverboards. Michael Rogers, one of the futurists quoted in this article, said that at least the movie "wasn't a scary dystopia" and another, Ross Dawson, said, "we discover what we want."

Predictions of Futurists

Predicting future consequences from analysis of present-day events has been the major concern of the World Future Society, founded in 1967. Members of this group are drawn from many professions but all members attempt to use scientific reasoning to forecast what short-term and long-term future scenarios will be. In a recent publication entitled *Outlook 2015*, the "Top Trends and Forecasts for the Decade Ahead" suggested that the technological changes already developed will lead to vast societal differences even in the next 10 to 30 years. Some of the predictions from this issue include the following:

> Advances in artificial intelligence are improving manufacturing and leading to economic growth but this change will require fewer human workers. By enabling computer-controlled creatures to gain brains comparable to human ones, these independent-living emulations of human beings (ems) could do most of the work of society. This result would affect employment because humans would need technical capabilities that relate to innovation rather than routine performance.
>
> Robotic exoskeletons that fit over the bodies of soldiers for protection or of older persons who need physical movement assistance will be available. Medicine may rely on digestible sensors that report on human's health status, prosthetics will feel like human body parts, human organs will be manufactured, and genomes will be altered to enable humans to thwart the aging process.
>
> Computers now can understand human words more clearly and they could be used as "spying machines." Because computer chips will be the size of grains of sand, they will be everywhere collecting data and aerial drones will be pervasive. There may be brain-wave detectives in courtrooms instead of juries, driverless cars will make insurance unnecessary, and "temporal prediction" algorithms will predict traffic, crimes, and civil disturbances.

These sets of predictions are still relatively short term but in his books on this topic one of the founders of the World Future Society, Ray Kurzweil (2005) has predicted that by 2020 there will be accurate computer simulations of the human brain and in the longer term (post 2045), creatures of technology (e.g., nanobots) will begin to take over the human world. This "singularity" will occur gradually as various parts of the human body and brain become augmented by technology. He predicts that as these technology-generated beings continue to gain the cognitive skills of humans, the human brain and body will cease to exist. Thus, human/tech creatures will never die. There are many other futurists who are concerned about Kurzweil's prediction, however, and they suggest that this trend must be addressed and, if not desired, changed.

Bill Joy, who is cofounder of Microsystems, stated in 2000, "The new Pandora's boxes of genetics, nanotechnology, and robotics are almost open, yet we seem hardly to have noticed. Ideas can't be put back in a box . . . Once they are out, they are out" (p. 68). He suggests that humans must address these issues to avoid some dire consequences, but also quotes Danny Hillis, cofounder of Thinking Machines Corporation and a futurist, who responded to these predictions by saying that the changes will be gradual so humans will just get used to them over time. Joy believes that these new technologies also hold "untold promise" but that with each one, power is accumulated by a smaller number of people. Although he says that could be dangerous, he says, "I remain optimistic" (p. 73).

It is beyond the purview of this book to discuss possible effects of all of these technological changes on future human experience. However, because the types of play in which children engage have such powerful effects on their developmental trajectories, an issue of great interest is whether and how changes in children's play behaviors resulting from their pervasive use of technology-augmented play materials may become factors affecting human brain development and other human abilities in this century and beyond.

Potential Effects of Technology-Augmented Play on Brain Maturation and on Social, Emotional, Moral, and Cognitive Development

In an essay entitled "Play and the Origin of the Species" Michael Ellis (1998) asserted that human evolution has been shaped and fostered by our species' propensity for play. He suggested that although play is not necessary for human survival on an immediate basis, it has been crucial for evolutionary survival because human playfulness extends the limits of human experiences and enables us to be capable of dealing with future unknowns. He concluded, "It brought us to where we are now both as a species and as individuals and will be the basis for our future adaptation to the unpredictable future" (p. 31). Thus, it is possible that the technology-augmented play experiences of children and adolescents today will prepare them for a future with increased human possibilities or that such play will fit them for a future with diminished human possibilities. It is also possible that the effects of such play will be more radical at some age periods than at other age periods because of the types of brain development going on at those age periods.

Potential Effects of Technology-Augmented Play on Infants and Young Children

Because the growth and elaboration of the neuronal network are at their peak during the first 5 years of life, the experiences that young children encounter will have a major effect on how their brains develop and on which networks and functional areas of their brains are most richly structured. Reviewing this information, during the first year of life the somatosensory, vestibular, and motor systems develop rapidly. As noted earlier, infants thrive on being touched and by being able to touch other people and objects in the environment, and they also love being bounced, swung, and given other vestibular experiences (Eliot, 1999). The coordination of voluntary movement increases as the cerebellum and basal ganglia areas are myelinated. The amygdala, site of emotional responses, is already active and within the first year, the limbic cortex matures so that expressions of attachment and stranger anxiety are seen. Infants are also extremely responsive to speech and by 1 year they are more responsive to the language sounds of their native environment.

In a recent book concerned with the value of face-to-face interpersonal interactions, Susan Pinker (*The Village Effect*, 2014) reminds the reader that human babies are "hardwired to connect face-face" (p. 126); that is, their brains are already prepared to observe parents' and other humans' social engagement with them and to respond with imitative behaviors. She cites Meltzoff and colleagues (Saby, Marshall, & Meltzoff, 2012; Saby, Meltzoff, & Marshall, 2013), who have studied infant/parent social interaction extensively, and who recently described the brain mapping and mirror neuron activity occurring in infants when they have participated in child/parent socially playful interactions. During such interactions, the infant brain is extremely active and reflects dynamic connective actions in many areas. These researchers suggest that these early brain mappings may be predictive of infant social attachment. Whether the same types of mappings will occur when infants interact with technology-augmented toys, phones, tablets, or robotic creatures is presently unknown. Pinker (2014) cites many examples, however, of how technology has changed the "face-to-face" interactions that were prominent in pretechnology eras.

As discussed earlier, the first representative mode identified by Bruner (1964) involves *enactive* cognition, which is facilitated by motoric and social interactions of young children with other humans in their environment. Presently it is not known how much of such "real-world" interaction is needed in order for optimal brain, social, and cognitive development, but it is possible that this developmental process will be affected profoundly if very young children spend less time in human social and play engagement and more time in technology-augmented play engagement. An interesting study that involved a toddler engaged in CD-ROM play showed that after the child had learned to click to play it, he then began to "click" his parents to get them to do the things he desired, showing that the interactive behavior with the device carried over to behavior with humans (Smith, 2002). Evidence from young children raised long term in socially deficient environments (e.g., Carlson & Earls, 1997) where human care, contact, and interaction are minimal indicates that these children's brain development, social skills, and cognition all are negatively affected. Because technology-augmented devices such as cell phones and electronic tablets provide iconic rather than enactive cognitive experiences, young children who spend a greater proportion of time interacting with such devices rather than being engaged in enactive social experiences with parents, teachers, siblings, or other children may have brains that are structured differently or less richly and thus their developmental progress might have some characteristics of young children who have been raised in socially deficient environments.

It also is presently unclear whether there will be differences in young children's brain development if early experiences are primarily with virtual materials that emphasize iconic and symbolic interactions. However, it is already common for parents to report that their children, who have had electronic phone or tablet experiences, press their finger on the TV screen or on pictures in magazines, thinking that the images can be activated that way. Thus, their interactive motor schemes seemed to have been affected by their technology-augmented experiences. If one of the potential effects of a technology-augmented environment is the diminishment of time spent in human interactions, children might have different configurations of the parts of the brain that encode social and emotional behavior, as well as different cognitive understanding of those behaviors. If, as Bruner suggested, enactive cognition is the first step in higher orders of cognition, the diminishment or reconfiguration of enactive cognition may result in other cognitive variations. The theorists who have discussed "embodied cognition" have speculated that sensorimotor experiences may underlie cognitive processes at all age levels (Wilson, 2002). Thus, the loss of such "real-world" cognition could have effects not only in early childhood but at all age levels. A recent study (Jirout & Newcombe, 2015) of parents' reports of their 4- to 7-year-olds' types of play supports this view. The researchers found that the children's amount of spatial play (i.e., playing with puzzles, blocks, and board games) was positively associated with their spatial cognitive skills even when other variables such as gender, socioeconomic status, family income and education, and general intelligence were controlled.

During the preschool age period, growth in social and emotional control, as well as moral, language, and cognitive understanding are extensive, and synaptic density continues to increase, indicating that with every experience, young children's brains are becoming more densely configured. Thus, whatever experiences they are having, whether it is pretending with dolls, blocks, and cars, or pressing electronic tablets to see designs or activate actions, their brains will be incorporating these experiences and neuronal connections will be getting stronger in those areas where the most action is occurring. Recent research to improve Head Start children's emotional understanding and control has shown that a method involving active learning through structured "make-believe" play activities produced positive impacts on the children's emotion knowledge but did not improve their executive functioning skills (Morris et al., 2014). Whether longer-term imaginative play would increase these control skills is presently unknown, and whether exposure to emotionally focused content on digital devices would affect such skills is in need of research. However, the themes of the pretense also are crucial because there is a great deal of research showing that children who watch violent television and online programs are more likely to have violent themes in their play (Levin, 2013, 2015).

Cognitive processes such as memory development have extensive growth during the preschool years as the primary brain areas for memory activation mature and become myelinated. Because young children's brains engage in making synaptic connections with their every experience, it is reasonable to conclude that the brains of children who have play experiences that are different from the play of children in the past will be configured differently. These new configurations may be useful in the future society; however, whether behaviors that are useful in natural environments or in nonvirtual human interactions will be lost as such technological experiences become even more pervasive is a question of interest. Recently the Sesame Workshop (Neary, 2014) created a game called "Big Bird's Words," designed for smartphones, which is an app that turns into a "wordascope." The goal is to show children how words are related by having a "word tree." When children access some words, other related words also appear. Designers expect the game to require some parent involvement with the smartphone to prevent its use "as a baby sitter." This concern is prevalent in the view of child development specialists because they are concerned that parent-child interaction will diminish if these media supplant human interaction.

According to Lee (2015), early childhood educators also will need to make some revisions in their teaching methods in order to use digital media effectively. Lee states that, because these media now are "pervasive" in young children's lives and they generate high levels of child interest, they can increase the motivation for learning for children from all backgrounds. If learning can be more engaging and enjoyable through the use of technology-augmented playful devices, children's ability to attend to and gain understanding of academic skills in particular might increase. Lee gives examples of how such devices can be used in playful ways both with individual children and small groups while also maintaining appropriate levels of educator-child-child interactions.

In regard to the affordances of these digital devices, although the behaviors used to activate such technology-augmented play materials may be transparent in relation to the device features, this type of transparency may not be relevant for helping children understand or engage in human social interaction behaviors. The devices also may provide narrower challenge experiences than traditional play materials and be less socially accessible, providing diminished social experiences with other humans. In particular, a pervasive technology-augmented environment during the earliest period of brain development may result in human brains that are more responsive to technological interactions than to human interactions. Certainly, this would not occur with moderate use of such devices as long as there were still many opportunities for human enactive experiences as well as iconic and symbolic ones. However, if such interactive devices replace human interaction, there could be definite consequences on early brain development and subsequently on human social, emotional, moral, and cognitive development.

Presently there is no long-term research that can shed light on the effects of these newest technology-augmented devices. However, there are some reports of long-term cognitive and social effects of extensive television exposure. For example, Lillard and Peterson (2011) found differences in preschool children's planning and self-control abilities when they experienced fast-paced television cartoons as compared with slower educational programs and picture drawing. Another study that examined relationships between exposure to violent television viewing when children were 2 to 5 years of age and their antisocial behavior at ages 7 to 10 found that for boys, there was a relationship. Viewing of violent programming by preschool boys was associated with subsequent aggressive behavior (Christakis & Zimmerman, 2007). Longitudinal studies of such differences among children with high and low exposure to technology-augmented toys, electronic tablets, and other virtual media are needed in order to understand the possible differences in brain development in the future. One possibility is that they will be more effectively adapted to a world where virtual experiences and technology-augmented devices are pervasively used. For example, when they grow old they may be more open to having robot caregivers (Aronson, 2014). Especially in early childhood there is no question that the dynamic systems of brain development, play development, and technology innovation will be affected by these changes, especially in regard to such dynamic factors as sensitive dependence on initial conditions, phase shifts, nonlinearity, plasticity, recursion, and attractor states.

Much will depend on what mix of play experiences young children continue to enjoy. If technology-augmented play enlarges their repertoire of social behaviors and cognitive skills in the virtual and symbolic dimensions but they continue to maintain enough "real-world" enactive experiences to keep them learning from those experiences, then their brains may be even more richly connected and their potential creative thought even more elaborated. However, if these newer types of play supplant earlier ones, then their brains may be designed quite differently from those of children of the past, although appropriately configured for the future.

Potential Effects of Technology-Augmented Play on Development of Older Children and Adolescents

As noted earlier, although the primary period for brain synaptogenesis and initial pruning occurs during early childhood, the age periods from 6 to 12 and from 13 to 21 also are ones in which play activities and other experiences can strongly affect brain development. During the childhood age period synaptogenesis and myelination continue to occur, although not at the same pace as in earlier years. At about age 7 the frontal lobe is at its highest synaptic density and pruning of brain areas that are used less extensively begins to occur. Memory and other intellectual processes such as problem solving gain in speed and efficiency as myelination and pruning advance. More individualization of brain structures occur during this period as children's experiences become more focused. During this period, the range, intensity, and types of children's experiences can influence the brain's growth in many areas, such as number of dendrites, configuration of synapses, and processes of myelination (Eliot, 1999).

In the years before puberty, there is a peak in growth rates of the association and language cortical areas, and the corpus callosum, which connects the brain hemispheres, also grows extensively. According to Thompson and Nelson (2001), "The brain regions most relevant to higher cognition, including reasoning and problem solving, self-regulation, personality, and strategic functioning, have a maturational course extending into adolescence"(p. 10). The areas of the adolescent brain that are not completely mature include the insula and others areas of the limbic system such as the amygdala and hippocampus. Since these areas are related to emotional control, risk assessment, and emotional reactivity, they may be especially sensitive to experiences that involve those types of skills (Baird et al., 1999), and technology-augmented play that focuses on activities related to these areas of the brain may be more likely to affect brain development in later childhood and adolescence.

Because pruning also becomes extensive during this period and the more-often-used skills or activities gain stronger connections while less-used ones do not maintain strong brain connections, the range of playful experiences and consequent breadth of social, emotional, and cognitive growth may differ greatly among elementary age children and adolescents. When this specialization occurs, those with high- or low-technology-augmented play or different types of such play (e.g., creative programming, violent video games, Instagram use) all may have brains that are configured in quite different ways.

There are a number of potential social, emotional, moral, and cognitive developmental issues that may be affected by extensive use of augmented play materials. Some of these have potentially positive and some potentially negative consequences. Attributes such as empathy may be reduced when it is so easy for the individuals to detach from reality and embody a virtual existence. Their increased ability to compartmentalize experiences thus may reduce their need to consider others or to engage in activities related to the "common good." In particular, children who may have difficulties in other areas of their lives may think, "no worries because I'll just go home and play 'The Sims' on my computer." Instead of grappling with day-to-day issues and mastering problems that need to be addressed, it is tempting to "live another life" on the computer. Not surprisingly, the fantasy game Kim Kardashian: Hollywood™ in which players live glamorous virtual lives is "among the top 10 most recently downloaded apps for the iPhone, according to Apple" (Wortham, 2014).

Reports of bullying and social exclusion on various social media venues also have become of concern (see Hinduja & Patchin, 2007; Juvonen & Gross, 2008; Katzer, Fetchenhauer, & Belschak, 2009) and it seems that when social experiences are virtual rather than in face-to-face social settings, young people have more difficulty in evaluating the effects of their social and emotional responses. For example, there is evidence that even young girls may show "relational aggression" that involves excluding other girls from friendships (Reddy, 2014). This behavior appears to be greatly extended in much online communication, especially among girls. Similarly there has been concern expressed about young people supplanting physical encounters with "virtual quasi relations," including online casual sex (Wayne, 2014). When young people spend less time in the enactive "real-world" level of interaction, their ability to be synchronized in communication and emotional tone may be more difficult. On the other hand, if virtual interactions will become the more common mode of playful interaction, perhaps these skills will be learned and better communicated in virtual environments.

Perhaps their early childhood technology-augmented play will increase the likelihood that older children will choose virtual experiences in lieu of real experiences, leading to a reduction in their valuing of real-world experiences. For example, they may question why it would be good to go camping when bugs might be present, learn to ski or swim since these activities take physical practice, or even play games outside with other children. Piaget's view (1965) that higher levels of moral development are gained by child-child discussions of fairness during their game play would suggest that if children grow up without the opportunity to engage in face-to-face interactions that permit discussions of the fairness of the rules of their social games, their moral development and the values of the society might be negatively affected. Similarly, children may grow into adults who think that the virtual tour of the Machu Picchu is a replacement for the real experience. Even more significant is the idea that when the opportunity to visit Machu Picchu presents itself, the individuals are likely to refuse on the basis of prior experience, albeit via the virtual tour. In essence, they would believe "I've already seen that."

As children and adolescents rely more and more on virtual experiences such as texting, blogging, and gaming, they may become less physically active and their social experiences may consist entirely of virtual interactions. This has already been a concern in television viewing and computer use (Wake, Hesketh, & Waters, 2003). Bauerlein (2008) has expressed concern that technology-augmented devices used by adolescents have not expanded their range of experiences but rather they have "contracted the horizon to themselves and the social scene around them" (p. 10). That is, he sees these adolescents as living in their own virtual world of social media, gaming, and superficial reading, which is thus isolating them from the culture of the larger society. He characterizes this world as "impoverished" rather than being expansive and growth producing. He concludes that present day young adults already are the "dumbest generation" because of their pervasive use of virtual rather than actual experiences.

A recent report in the *New York Times* (Wingfield, 2014) indicated that in the United States, fans of gaming are becoming avid spectators by watching E-Sports rather than playing themselves. They fill theaters to watch experts play other experts! This trend is also occurring in South Korea, indicating that even the activity of gaming is beginning to be a passive spectator sport with only "experts" playing the game (Wingfield, 2014). It is true that the new video gaming "sport" bears much similarity to any professional sport in terms of fans preferring to watch rather than play, as evidenced by the millions of "armchair quarterbacks" for American football. It is also true that cultural changes sometimes create uncertainty and fear, as exemplified by the Luddites. Thus, it may be that there is currently an overreaction to the idea of the video game culture becoming a more prominent feature in society. However, one argument against the rise of the gaming culture is that unlike other physical activities, young people can literally play video games all day and all night. Hence, the virtual experience has the potential to (and does so frequently) displace all other activities, both physical and otherwise. Normally, other sports involve limitations such as fatigue, but digital games, and to a large extent online play environments, have much fewer factors that force limits on how much an individual can engage in the task. Digital games and online play environments allow users to play until the proverbial "cows come home." What the effect of such experiences will be on executive functioning skills such as planning and self-regulation is unknown at this time.

It is certainly possible, however, that technology-augmented play will have a role in enhancing older children's creative and other cognitive skills. One proponent of technology who sees this possibility is Mitchel Resnick of the MIT Media Laboratory. In a recent chapter (Resnick, 2006) he said that computers should be thought of more as "paintbrushes" rather than as "television sets" because they are really a "medium for creative design and expression" (p. 192). He thinks that even though many adults see them as stifling creativity, he has an "alternate vision" and he describes a project in which children were encouraged to engage in designing machines and the computer programs that could operate them. Resnick is concerned about the polarization of opinions regarding technology-augmented play and comments, "we need to focus on the difference between activities that foster creative thinking and creative expression (whether they use high-tech, low-tech, or not-tech) and those that don't" (p. 204).

One overwhelmingly positive outcome of the current situation, especially in terms of digital games and the "sports" being created, is the reduced emphasis on traditional male qualities such as strength and speed. It may be that the gaming "sport" is democratized at least for females, because there is no physical barrier to competing. This may also be the case for those with certain disabilities. According to Dell, Newton, and Petroff (2011), various types of assistive technologies can greatly expand both the educational and play experiences of children and adolescents with disabilities. Thus, technology may be a great source for increasing the active involvement of those with physical disabilities, in particular.

The issue of virtual experiences versus real experiences is also one that must be addressed by schools and colleges. Researchers interested in how well students learned information in college classes have found that although students who used computers to take notes did as well on factual test-taking items as did physical writing note-takers they performed less well on conceptual application questions (Mueller & Oppenheimer, 2014). It may be possible that memory storage may also be affected because with the advent of the internet most needed information can be found quickly rather than needing to be recalled from human memory. This is not the first time technological invention has affected memory. Foer (2011) has discussed how human memory activity changed with the invention of writing and reading because before that time, at least some community members (professional memorizers) carried extensive mental information about the entire history and relevant factual information of their society. Another cognitive skill affected by recent technology may be spatial knowledge of geographic features, which now may also be less detailed because of the extensive use of GPS systems. Rather than adults constructing map-like mental images of geographic space, even their spatial images may be more like those of young children who typically draw maps in relation to themselves, showing the personal route they have taken, that is, through the hall, through the living room, through the kitchen (Piaget & Inhelder, 1956).

Whether moral development will be negatively affected by virtual experiences is also a question of interest (Bergen & Davis, 2011; Bergen & Davis, 2013; Davis & Bergen, 2014), as many theorists have proposed strong theoretical links between social game play and moral issues, as well as experiences solving moral dilemmas in pretense. At least some studies have reported a possible diminishment of moral qualities. For example, a meta-analysis study by Konrath, O'Brien, and Hsing (2010) found that college students do not have as much empathy as they used to have, and they speculate that this loss is tied to the rise of electronic media use, which may cause young people "to care more about themselves and to interact less with real others" (p. 10). Gentile and Gentile (2008) have stated that moral behavior goals such as sharing, tolerance, and peaceful ways to resolve conflicts are in competition with goals from video games that encourage values such as "competition, aggression, acquisitiveness, and lust" (p. 137).

There are also current educational trends that are at the intersection of play and learning. Game-based learning, game design, gamification, as well as some forms of online learning seek to integrate various ideas about play into formal learning environments, although each of these approaches is distinct about which elements of games and play are integrated. Both game-based learning and game design directly involve digital games in an educational setting. Game-based learning often emphasizes the learning that is inherent within game play, such as with a player of "Call of Duty" who will develop historical knowledge in order to succeed in the game. By contract, game-design initiatives often emphasize the knowledge and skills that are required, and thus developed, through the process of creating a new game that may include technological knowledge as skills (e.g., coding), computation skills, or knowledge of a particular subject matter relevant to the game design. Gamification, however, does not include digital games specifically. Gamification is the integration of game-play elements in a formal learning environment. In a "gamified" class, for example, a student may not complete an assignment for a letter grade, but rather would complete a "level" in order to advance to the next level in the class, a transition known as "leveling up." Many online learning resources also use elements of games or principles of gamification by designing learning activities around earning "badges" that represent an acquired skill or competency. In many cases, these digital "badges" are considered real-world credentials of a particular skill.

The integration and intersection between games and learning can have both positive and negative influence on learning and brain development. On one hand, using elements of game play to enhance engagement in the learning process can be a very powerful educational tool. However, this also requires creativity, knowledge, and experience in areas that may not be widely valued for educators as well as flexibility within the learning environment that is often limited due to current trends towards increased testing and measurement. In order to successfully integrate games and learning, educators must be able to address Resnick's (2006) call to see technology game play more as a means of enhancing creativity rather than a means of controlling thinking. For example, game play in a game such as Minecraft that has no predefined objective is drastically different than game play in other genres. Further, knowledge and skills that are gained through designing a game is vastly different than what may be gained through more traditional learning environments. Understanding the ways in which learning occurs differently through game play is essential to successful use of games or game-play concepts in teaching and learning environments.

The factors that influence the meaningful use of technologies such as digital games in teaching and learning has be explored from perspectives such as the Technological Pedagogical Content Knowledge (TPACK) framework (Koehler & Mishra, 2009) and self-efficacy beliefs regarding technology use in teaching and learning (Abbitt, 2011; Abbitt & Klett, 2007; Albion, 1999, 2001). Undoubtedly, there are many factors that influence the ways in which educators consider technology-enhanced learning. With respect to digital games and learning, it is expected that the ways in which learning will benefit from games and game-based learning will change dramatically if those who are entering the field of education are also active "gamers" with personal experience in the playing of games that informs their concept of a meaningful learning environment.

Technology-Augmented Play as Preparation for a Different Future

It also could be the case that the technology-augmented play environment will enhance human abilities that are needed in the future and create a more positive world for all humans. For example, current play with technology-augmented playthings may be very beneficial because individuals may develop proficiency in both the real and virtual worlds, and have the ability to move seamlessly between environments and also use the capabilities of one to test for the other. Thus, if individuals are socially introverted, they might use video games such as The Sims as a testing area to experiment or try different activities and personas, in an effort to see the consequences. This play might inform them about what may or may not be advisable in the real world. One instance where the virtual world informed the real world was in a "Corrupted Blood" incident in the game World of Warcraft. In this instance, a glitch in the game resulted in the spread of a plague, the result of which drew stark comparisons to what would happen if a similar event happened in real life (Lofgren & Fefferman, 2007). This game incident prompted scholars to look seriously at the virtual world as a possible testing area for dealing with real-world phenomena.

Similarly, video games have been shown to have a positive effect on response time (Dye et al., 2009). Technology-focused play also might enhance performance in physical activities such as sports. That is, games may act as viable models for young athletes to follow. For example, given the popularity and fidelity of games such as the FIFA and Madden NFL series from EA Sports, it is conceivable that, controlling for confounding variables, athletes playing these video games might perform better than those who do not play these games. Research has already shown that video games can have benefits in terms of visual processing (Green & Bavelier, 2007), but they may also provide benefits in terms of overall performance. Because high-fidelity sports-related video games have technical and tactical advantages that illustrate what is technically possible and effective (i.e., in moves by the exceptional players), they can allow the ordinary player to make tactical choices that can then be interpreted and executed in real-life matches. The video games in this case act as models for performance and motivation when young players have video game experiences and then try to create similar experiences in the real world. A number of recent articles have also pointed out training for war has changed with the advent of technology-augmented devices.

Technology has a significant effect on many aspects of human life, including warfare (Miller, 2012). The U.S. military is tremendously capable in part because it has access to advanced technologies that allow it to accomplish tasks that other countries cannot. Soldiers in the U.S. military, consequently, have additional requirements because they must be able to effectively use technologies that give them an advantage in the field. Interacting with these technologies is extremely important and it is might be the case that soldiers who grew up in technology-rich environments might be more suited to modern warfare systems that are technology-intensive. An example is the Common Remotely Operated Weapons Station, or CROWS 2 system, which allows soldiers to remain safe within an armored structure while controlling the weapon system remotely. The control and interaction are based on the video-game metaphor, but the consequences of using the system are very real. It is conceivable that current play with technology-augmented playthings will result in individuals specifically adapted to using those tools in the future. For example, one study indicated that video game experience enhanced participants' performance on combat identification tasks (Keebler et al., 2014) Thus, future soldiers will possess the required skills necessary to function on the technology- and media-rich battlefield of future.

However, the psychological costs will probably be as much an issue then as it is now. Currently, there is much concern about the remote warfare capabilities of the U.S. military and the effect it has on soldiers. For example, research involving pilots of unmanned aerial vehicles or "drones" have shown that they are susceptible to Post-Traumatic Stress Disorder (PTSD) despite the fact that they are not necessarily in harm's way (Chappelle et al., 2014; Miller, 2012). In essence, current play involving technology might select a developmental path suited for the future battlefield, but it is unclear that current play will also select a path where individuals develop the emotional structures necessary to cope with the future battlefield.

Play has the potential to change the brain, and humans have the ability to purposefully change the environment. It is thus prudent, given current play patterns, to consider what the future might be like in terms of physical and social structures. From a physical standpoint, questions of representation may become important as the virtual world becomes more ubiquitous and more accepted as "real." For example, in a future populated by technology-motivated individuals, it might be commonplace for students to attend a class lecture delivered by a hologram of the professor. Or, individuals may be comfortable maintaining a long-distance relationship using a humanoid robot under the control of the remotely located partner. In this case, the robot is acting as a proxy for a real human, performing all associated tasks. There are already "smart home" technologies being marketed.

Social structures may also be significantly changed given current patterns of technology-mediated play. Future societies may grapple with issues such as the "rights" of an avatar or virtual persona. Although there is growing concern regarding issues such as identity theft, there is less concern over issues such as theft of virtual goods, particularly when crimes are committed within a game environment. Future societies will need to answer questions involving virtual property and the idea of culpability in the virtual world. Issues become even more complex when artificial intelligence is considered. Future societies may need to be comfortable with the idea of artificially intelligent agents receiving credit and being held accountable for actions performed in either the real or virtual world.

Defining the Future

In the book *Brave New World* (Huxley, 1932), a society is described in which only a small number of individuals are involved in creative, productive, and decision-making work while the rest of the caste-like population is "happily" controlled by drugs and socially managed activities. Similarly, in the movie *Wall-E*, most humans are passive drone-like creatures just concerned with their own pleasures. Some of the more recent predictions of the world of the future suggest that only those humans with high levels of technology skills will have creative and productive lives, while the rest of the human species will be controlled by technological devices. Whether the trends in technology-augmented play are leading to such a division in human society is unknown at this time. However, the potential long-term effects of pervasive levels of technology-augmented play are in need of much research and discussion. As noted earlier, when predicting the future, the salience and strength of various data points can vary greatly in the futurists' view. Thus, the negative perspectives of some writers may be giving too much weight to factors that may not be as powerful as other more positive factors and vice versa.

There are many future predictions that envision a wonderful world enhanced by technological advances. For example, Scott (2014) envisions a world that has a range of useful or even "magical" technologies that could solve the world hunger problem, reverse aging, and free humans of the "archaic idea" of work. He suggests that the future might result in humans being relieved of all onerous activities and being enabled to focus their lives on artistic, cognitive, and scientific pursuits. Scott indicates that the future will be formed by humans visualizing their desires and preferences, as well as their fears, and suggests that in the coming years, the ways humans visualize their desires, preferences, and fears will be major factors in determining how such expanding technology affects human play and subsequently human brain development, social interactions, emotional life, moral choices, and cognitive powers.

A central point of the authors of this book is that the expanding technology that has created many new and enhanced play opportunities for children is influencing traditional aspects of the play of infants, young children, older children, and adolescents and thus, it will be affecting their developmental trajectories potentially in both positive and negative ways. The task of parents, educators, toy product designers, virtual play creators, and the community as a whole is to be cognizant of such effects, to continually monitor the effects, and to try to make these new play opportunities brain developmentally rich and growth-enhancing as well as relevant for the world of the future.

FIGURE 5.1 Just checking the latest Pinterest!

FIGURE 5.2 I'm contacting all my friends on Instagram.

FIGURE 5.3 This is my favorite computer game.

FiGURE 5.4 Engaged with my favorite Xbox game.

Activities and Questions for Discussion

1. Select one example of a technology-augmented play material that young children can presently use and describe the representation modes and affordances that are primary in play with this toy. Then speculate about the effects of that play on their brain development, social or emotional behaviors, and cognition. Evaluate whether and how such play will prepare them for living in the future of human society.

2. Select one example of an online game or other online experience that older children can presently use and describe the representation modes and affordances that are primary in play with this experience. Then speculate about the effects of that play on their brain development, social or emotional behaviors, and cognition. Evaluate whether and how such play will prepare them for living in the future of human society.

3. Evaluate your own play experiences with technology-augmented play materials or virtual experiences and speculate on what about these experiences have made you better prepared for future society and/or made your development diminished in some way. If such diminishment has occurred, suggest ways to change your play to enhance your developmental opportunities.

References

Abbitt, J.T. (2011). An investigation of the relationship between self-efficacy beliefs about technology integration and technological pedagogical content knowledge (TPACK) among preservice teachers. *Journal of Digital Learning in Teacher Education, 27*(4), 134–143.

Abbitt, J.T., and Klett, M. (2007). Identifying influences on attitudes and self-efficacy beliefs towards technology integration among pre-service educators. *Electronic Journal for the Integration of Technology in Education, 5,* 28–42.

Albion, P. (1999). Self-efficacy beliefs as an indicator of teachers' preparedness for teaching with technology. Paper presented at the Society for Information Technology and Teacher Education Conference, Norfolk, VA. http://www.editlib.org/index.cfm/files/paper_8156.pdf?fuseaction=Reader.DownloadFullText&paper_id=8156

Albion, P.R. (2001). Some factors in the development of self-efficacy beliefs for computer use among teacher education students. *Journal of Technology and Teacher Education, 9*(3), 321–347.

Aronson, L. (2014). The future of robot cargivers. *New York Times,* 7/20, p. 4 sr.

Baird, A.A., Gruber, S. A, Fein, D.A., Maas, L.C., Steingard, R.J., & Renshaw, J.F. (1999). Functional magnetic resonance imaging of facial affect recognition in children and adolescents. *Journal of the American Academy of Child and Adolescent Psychiatry, 2,* 195–199.

Bauerlein, M. (2008). *The dumbest generation: How the digital age stupefies young Americans and jeopardizes our future (or, don't trust anyone under 30).* New York: Penguin.

Bergen, D. & Davis, D. (2011). Influences of technology-related playful activity and thought on moral development. *American Journal of Play, 4*(1), 80–99.

Bergen, D. & Davis, D. (2013). Playful activity and thought as the medium for moral development: Implications for moral education. In B.J. Irby, G. Brown, R. Lara-Alecio, &

S. Jackson (Eds.) and R.A. Robles-Piñã (Sect. Ed.), *The handbook of educational theories* (pp. 653–666). Charlotte, NC: Information Age Publishing, Inc.

Bradbury, R. (1953/1991). *Fahrenheit 451*. New York: Del Rey.

Bruner, J.S. (1964). The course of cognitive growth. *American Psychologist, 19*(1), 1–15.

Burgess, A. (1962/1987). *A clockwork orange*. (Reprint). New York: W.W. Norton.

Butler S. (1921). *Erewhon*. London: Jonathan Cape.

Carlson, M., & Earls, F. (1997). Psychological and neuroendocrinolgical sequelae of early social deprivation in institutionalized children in Romania. In C.S. Carter, I.I. Lederhendler, & B. Kirkpatrick (Eds.), *The integrative Eurobiology of affiliation* (pp. 419–428). New York: New York Academy of Sciences.

Chappelle, W., Swearengen, J., Goodman, T., & Thompson, W. (2014). *Personality Test Scores that Distinguish US Air Force Remotely Piloted Aircraft Drone Pilot Training Candidates* (No. AFRL-SA-WP-TR-2014–0001). School of Aerospace Medicine, Wright Patterson AFB.

Christakis, D.A., & Zimmerman, F.J. (2007). Violent television viewing during preschool is associated with antisocial behavior during school age. *Pediatrics, 120*(5), 993–999.

Davis, D., & Bergen, D. (2014). Relationships among play behaviors reported by college students and their responses to moral issues: A pilot study. *Journal of Research in Childhood Education, 28*, 484–498.

Dell, A.G., Newton, D., & Petroff, J.G. (2011). *Assistive technology in the classroom: Enhancing the school experiences of students with disabilities*. Boston: Pearson Higher Ed.

Dye, M., Green, S., & Bavelier, D. (2009). Increasing speed of processing with action video games. *Current Directions in Psychological Science, 18*(6), 321–326.

Eliot, L. (1999). *What's going on in there: How the brain and mind develop in the first five years of life*. New York: Bantam.

Ellis, M. J. (1998). Play and the origin of the species. In D. Bergen (Ed.), *Readings from play as a learning medium* (pp. 29-31). Olney, MD: ACEI.

Foer, J. (2011). *Moonwalking with Einstein: The art and science of remembering everything*. New York: Penguin.

Gentile, D. A., & Gentile, J. R. (2008). Violent Video Games as Exemplary Teachers: A Conceptual Analysis. *Journal of Youth and Adolescence, 37*(2), 127–141.

Green, C.S., & Bavelier, D. (2007). Action-video-game experience alters the spatial resolution of vision. *Psychological Science, 18*(1), 88–94.

Hinduja, S., & Patchin, J.W. (2007). Offline consequences of online victimization: School violence and delinquency. *Journal of School Violence, 6*(3), 89–112.

Huxley, A. (1932). *Brave new world*. London/Garden City, NY: Chatto & Windus/Doubleday, Doran & Co.

Jirout, J.J., & Newcombe, N.S. (2015). Building blocks for developing spatial skills: Evidence from a large, representative US sample. *Psychological Science*, 1–9.

Joy, B. (2000). Why the future doesn't need us. In F. Allhoff, P. Lin, J. Moor, & J. Weckert (Eds.), *Nanoethics–the ethical and social implicatons of nanotechnology* (pp. 17–39). Hoboken, NJ: John Wiley & Sons.

Juvonen, J., & Gross, E.F. (2008). Extending the school grounds?—Bullying experiences in cyberspace. *Journal of School Health, 78*(9), 496–505.

Katzer, C., Fetchenhauer, D., & Belschak, F. (2009). Cyberbullying: Who are the victims?: A comparison of victimization in internet chatrooms and victimization in school. *Journal of Media Psychology: Theories, Methods, and Applications, 21*(1), 25.

Keebler, J., Jentsch, F., & Schuster, D. (2014). The effects of video game experience and active stereoscopy on performance in combat identification tasks. *Human Factors, 56*(8), 1482–1496.

Koehler, M., & Mishra, P. (2009). What is technological pedagogical content knowledge? *Contemporary Issues in Technology and Teacher Education, 9*(1), 60–70.

Konrath, S.H., O'Brien, E.H., & Hsing, C. (2010). Changes in dispositional empathy in American college students over time: A meta-analysis. *Personality and Social Psychology Review, 15*, 180–198.

Kurzweil, R. (2005). *The singularity is near: When humans transcend biology.* New York: Penguin.

Lee, L. (2015). Young children, play, and technology: Meaningful ways of using technology and digital media. In D.P. Fromberg & D. Bergen (Eds.), *Play from birth to twelve* (3rd ed., pp. 217–224). New York: Routledge.

Levin, D. (2013). *Beyond remote-controlled childhood: Teaching young children in the media age.* Washington, DC: NAEYC.

Levin, D. (2015). Technology play concerns. In D. Fromberg & D. Bergen (Eds.) *Play from Birth to Twelve (3rd. ed)* (pp. 225–232). New York: Routledge.

Lillard, A.S., & Peterson, J. (2011). The immediate impact of different types of television on young children's executive function. *Pediatrics, 128*(4), 644–649.

Lofgren, E.T., & Fefferman, N. H. (2007). The untapped potential of virtual game worlds to shed light on real world epidemics. *The Lancet Infectious Diseases, 7*(9), 625–629.

Miller, A. (2012). A taxonomy of mixed reality visual displays. *IE-ICE Transactions on Information and Systems* (Special Issue on Networked Reality), vol. E77-D, no.12, 1321–1329, 1994.

More, T. (1516). *Utopia.* Oxford: University of Oxford.

Morris, P., Mattera, S.K., Castells, N., Bangser, M., Bierman, K., & Raver, C. (2014). Impact findings from the Head Start CARES Demonstration: National evaluation of three approaches to improving preschoolers' social and emotional competence. OPRE Report 2014–44. Washington, DC: Office of Planning, Research and Evaluation, Administration for Children and Families, U.S. Department of Health and Human Services.

Mueller, P.A., & Oppenheimer, D.M. (2014). The pen is mightier than the keyboard: Advantages of longhand over laptop note taking. *Psychological Science, 25*(6), 1159–1168.

Neary, L. (2014). Vocab-intensive for toddlers encourages anytime, anywhere learning. NPR, Dec. 31.

Orwell, G. (1949/1981). *Nineteen eighty-four.* New York: Signet.

Outlook 2015: Top trends and forecasts for the decade ahead. *The Futurist, 48*(6), 1–10.

Piaget, J. (1965). *The moral judgment of the child.* New York: Norton.

Piaget, J., & Inhelder, B. (1956). Child's conception of space. London: Routledge, Kegan Paul.

Pinker, S. (2014). *The village effect.* New York: Spiegel & Grau.

Plato. (380 BC). *Republic* (1974) translator G. M. A. Grube. Indianapolis: Hackett Publishing Co.

Reddy, S. (2014, May 27). Very little and acting mean. *Wall Street Journal*, pp. D1, D4.

Resnick, M. (2006). Computer as paintbush: Technology, play, and the creative society. In D. G. Singer, R. M. Golinkoff, & K. Hirsh-Pasek (Eds.), *Play = Learning: How play motivates and enhances children's cognitive and social-emotional growth.* New York: Oxford University Press.

Saby, J.N., Marshall, P.J., & Meltzoff, A.N. (2012). Neural correlates of being imitated: An EEG study in preverbal infants. *Social Neuroscience,* 7(6), 650–661.

Saby, J.N., Meltzoff, A.N., & Marshall, P.J. (2013). Infants' somatotopic neural responses to seeing human actions: I've got you under my skin. *PLOS ONE, 8*(10), e77905.

Schonfeld, Z. (2014, Dec. 18). Everything "Back to the Future Part II" got right and wrong about 2015, according to futurists. *Newsweek.* http://www.newsweek.com/everthing-back-future-ii-got-hilariously-wrong-about-2015-according-293272

Scott, G. (2014).Visualizing the future. *The Futurist, 48*(4), 20–23.

Smith, C.R. (2002). Click on me! An example of how a toddler used technology in play. *Journal of Early Childhood Literacy, 2*(1), 5–20.

Thompson, R.A. & Nelson, C.A. (2001). Developmental science and the media: Early brain development. *American Psychologist, 56*(1), 5–15.

Van Hise, J. (1992). *Man who created Star Trek: Gene Roddenberry.* Movie Publisher Services.

Wake, M., Hesketh, K., & Waters, E. (2003). Television, computer use and body mass index in Australian primary school children. *Journal of Paediatrics and Child Health, 39*(2), 130–134.

Wayne, T. (2014, Nov. 9) Swiping them off their feet. Future Tense, *New York Times,* p. 14.

We, Y. (1921/1924). *Zamyatin.* New York: E.P. Dutton.

Wilson, M. (2002). Six views of embodied cognition. *Psychonomic Bulletin & Review, 9*(4), 625–636.

Wingfield, N. (2014, Aug. 31).Virtual games draw real crowds and big money. *New York Times,* pp. 1, 13.

Wortham, J. (2014). Living like Kardashians, via Smartphone. *New York Times,* August 10, BU3.

6

FACILITATING OPTIMUM BRAIN MATURATION AND PLAY DEVELOPMENT IN A TECHNOLOGICALLY DIVERSE SOCIETY

Roles of Technology Designers, Community Stakeholders, Educators, and Parents

Professor Challenge accepted a buyout from Middle Country University even though she really was not ready to retire. However, her department courses now are all online and the university has decided that it is more cost effective just to keep the clinical faculty to maintain classes and interact online with students. Her husband, Professor Smarter, retired earlier when the Philosophy Department was reconceptualized into the Department of Technological Thought. Both parents are now wondering what is the best way to prepare their children, Blaine (age 4), Olivia (age 9), and Granson (age 15) to meet the employment and personal challenges of the future. They are aware that Blaine spends most play time in pretend activities with his talk/action figures or with animals that he has made from sticks and stones found in their yard. Olivia's play activities concern them because they involve extensive time in online communication with friends. She spends much time in her room since all of her schoolwork is also online. Granson primarily plays violent games online, but he also spends time hiking in the woods near their house and doing "extreme" sports with friends.

It is very difficult to make definitive recommendations about what the play of children and adolescents should be like and what the range of such play should incorporate given the present state of technology and the uncertainty of the future. Further complicating the issue is the fact that there are many diverging perspectives on what ought to happen and what should be the goals for society. These varied perspectives and the future predictions derived from those perspectives must be recognized as important because they will guide today's decisions that subsequently lay the groundwork for tomorrow's reality. The risks involved in encouraging certain types of play experiences rather than others is that if the encouraged behaviors are too narrow, parents and educators may be preparing young individuals for a society that will not exist. If they are too broad, however, then they may be so diffuse that they become meaningless. Nevertheless, the process of prediction and recommendation must occur because children of the future will be shaped by their play experiences just as children in the past were influenced by their play experiences. The play of infants, toddlers, and young children will clearly affect their brain development, as well as their social, emotional, moral, and cognitive development, and the play of older children and adolescents will be an important factor in promoting the refinement and strengthening of brain capabilities. Because the dynamic system interactions between play experiences and brain development are crucial elements for human survival and evolutionary success, preparing children for the future must involve attention to these issues.

One place to start is by determining the qualities that will benefit individuals despite whatever the future brings. Two such qualities are *versatility* and *resilience*. Versatile individuals can more easily adapt to future realities, and resilient individuals have the fortitude to recover from adversities. The important question thus becomes "How do we help foster versatility and resilience in younger individuals?" There are many ways to foster versatility and resilience but one of the most obvious ways is through their play. In particular, if during each age period of life, individuals have rich play experiences of all types, both traditional and technology-augmented, then the development of these characteristics will be greatly enhanced.

Playfulness is an advantage that human beings have in abundance and there is ample evidence of the evolutionary advantages of playfulness (Ellis, 1998; Smith, 2007). Combined with the human capacity for adaptation, it can be argued that effective forms of versatility and resilience could develop both from general, non-specific, play-related sources and from specifically designed play environments and materials of both non-technology and technology-augmented types. To encourage experiences that will prepare the next generations to have the versatility and resilience that they will need to meet ever-changing future environments, parents, educators, toy manufacturers, virtual game and online play designers, and interested adults in the community should all be aware of the changing play environment and try to promote a rich range of play experiences that will foster optimum brain development and effective adaptation to the world of the future.

Although the exact nature of the future world that humans will experience is unknown, one key to effective survival is through promoting the developmentally appropriate practices that parents and educators have promoted in the past while also supporting the expansion of abilities that may be required in the future.

Effective social, emotional, moral, and cognitive development will continue to rely on the versatility and resilience gained in play experiences during childhood and adolescence.

General Recommendations

Because of the rapidity of change in technology-augmented play and the potential interplay of this dynamic system with the dynamic systems of play development and brain maturation, it is not possible to give definitive short-term or long-term guidelines for how best to preserve the important qualities gained from play experiences. However, everyone who has responsibility for the future development of young children, older children, and adolescents can keep in mind the dynamic system factors that may interact to affect how well they are being prepared for their future. A review of some of these factors can give guidance for both practice and policy.

There are a number of the qualities of dynamic systems that must be kept in mind when planning and encouraging developmentally rich play experiences (Thelen & Smith, 1994). As noted earlier, such systems are:

> *Self-organizing*: Brain maturation exhibits *pattern and order that emerges from interactions* of many different components, including those that are part of the play development dynamic system. Although both of these systems will organize without having explicit instructions from the dynamic technological invention system, they will be influenced by such interactions, and the brain development process will use components from both typical play and technology-augmented play in its organizational efforts.
>
> *Nonlinear*: Because all of these processes are *unidirectional*, rather than linear (e.g., one cause ensures one effect), it is not possible to predict a one-to-one correspondence between specific play experiences and particular social, emotional, moral, or cognitive developmental outcomes for young children, older children, and adolescents. However, because the general brain maturation process is relatively well understood, it is possible to hypothesize that at certain ages, technology-augmented play of various types may be more or less influential on brain maturation, which will subsequently influence development in many areas.
>
> *Open*: Because all of these systems are organized by taking in *energy* from many sources, when new sources of technological experience are available, both brain and play systems will incorporate energy from technological advances and thus, be affected by such sources. However, since both are open systems, they will continue to incorporate energy from other societal aspects as well. The technological system also will be influenced by many sources. Thus, there will be dynamic synergy among all three systems.

Stable: All of these systems have *attractor* states in which the system establishes patterns of organization and, in those periods of time, assumptions may be made that a particular stable state will continue indefinitely. However, as soon as new energy or information is discovered or invented in one of these systems, the stability of the system will change and reorganization will occur. For example, the present technology-augmented play materials may change greatly in the future and thus the brain and play systems will experience changes if there are interactions with these technological reorganizations.

Changing: Systemic changes will continue to occur because in periods of *soft assembly* (when attractors are weak) there may be a greater impact from technology-augmented play than in more stable periods. Because of *sensitivity to initial conditions*, very small change processes can have major effects and often these are especially hard to predict. For example, the effect of electronic tablets on play seems to be great although, from a technological standpoint, this was not an extreme invention. On the other hand, very large technological change processes may not have such great effects on play. For example, television was a major invention and, although it changed some themes of children's pretend play, exposure to television did not affect children's ability to engage in pretense.

Complex with phase shifts: When there are periods of great change drawn from many sources, such as is the case presently, it is likely that phase shifts will occur. Because of extensive information from brain development research, expansion of play experiential components, and great speed of technology invention, there may be major systemic changes that will have long-term consequences on human social, emotional, moral, and cognitive development. Since a transition state is occurring presently, the present phase shift has not been completed.

Novelty-prone: One feature of dynamic systems that is always present is the great *flexibility*, especially for responding to novel conditions, that all three of these systems possess. Thus, the adaptive qualities of human brain maturation and play development will continue to expand and change as the impact of the technology-augmented play system becomes pervasive. Future brains and future play may have characteristics unforeseen at the present time as they adapt to the technology-augmented future.

Researchers already have used the dynamic systems model to study dyadic play (Steenbeck & van Geert, 2005) and have shown that self-organizing components of play systems change over time and follow many tenets of dynamic systems theory. For example, in a recent study of collaborative play, in which the dyadic interactions of the players were the variable of interest (Steenbeek, van der Aalsvoort, van Geert, 2014), the researchers found male and female differences in dyadic changes in the play system over time. They state that the purpose of such studies is "to try to understand the underlying dynamics of the play process by building a simulation model of these dynamics" (pp. 271–272). Similar studies involving children's social play with technology-augmented play materials are needed. As research techniques that draw on dynamic systems theory become more common in psychological and educational research, the many technological factors that are interacting to affect the dynamic system of the play and learning environment of the future may be more clearly identified. Until that is done, however, at least this dynamic perspective can be used to make recommendations for toy developers and marketers, digital game developers, online play environment designers, and community stakeholders, as well as for parents and educators.

Suggestions for Toy Developers and Marketers

It is important for adults who design and market toys, especially those with technology-augmented components to be aware of the dynamic system issues that are relevant for brain maturation and play development. In a recent chapter on emerging technology and toy design, Kudrowitz (2014) discusses the essentials of both technology-augmented and traditional types of toy design. First, he makes the distinction between a toy and a toy product. He says that toys can be any object, such as a spoon, that is played with but that "A toy product is an item that is intentionally designed for the primary purpose of play" (p. 237). He explains that those who design toys have special marketing problems. Toys must be innovative, robust, and relatively low cost and should appeal both to the children who will play with them and to the adults who will buy them. This market changes quickly and toy designers often do not have access to the most recently emerging technology. He suggests that toy designers need to think ahead to see how they will incorporate the newer technology into toys after it has been available in other products for some period of time. One of the ways that new technology is incorporated is by "wrapping" it around existing toys. For example, a software app might be downloaded to make a toy product be used in a new way or it may be controlled with a smartphone. Kudrowitz states that of the top 100 toys that sold in 2010, only about 10 of them had electronic components. As tablets and smart phones become typical playthings, however, he notes that the concept of a toy is changing. His advice to toy designers is to "make the toy about the play not about the technology. The play that the toy affords should be timeless" (p. 252).

There are some designers of technology-augmented play materials who try to embed the qualities of rich representation modes and affordances into their devices and games. For example, in Resnick's (2006) discussion of the creative possibilities of such play, he describes technology-augmented computer play that encourages creative designing by children. Another set of designers, Lund and colleagues (Lund, Klitbo, & Jessen, 2005; Lund & Marti, 2009) have addressed the enactive mode issue by developing Playware, which is a set of robotic building blocks that children move on and experience balancing from the feedback of the motion. The blocks are "intelligent" in that they are flexible and adaptive depending on children's movements. They state that those who design play materials for playgrounds should "adopt a design principle that respects this body-brain interplay" (Lund, Klitbo, & Jessen, 2005, p. 167). Such designs result in "children moving, exchanging, experimenting, and having fun, regardless of their cognitive or physical ability levels" (p. 168). Others have involved children not just in responding to technology but in being engaged in designing it. One of the greatest advocates for this approach is Allison Druin (2009, 2010) who involves children as "co-designers" of new technology. For example, Druin and Hendler (2000) have described a robot design program for elementary-age children, in which the children create the robotic toys.

In a study of children's play with "smart" plush toys that interfaced with computer programs, Luckin, Connolly, Plowman, and Airey (2003) found that children could master the varied interfaces between the two and did seek help when needed. However, they concluded that these types of toys "are not impressive as collaborative learning partners" (p. 1). In another discussion of "smart toys" Allen (2004) states that they have a few limitations at the present time. One limitation is that the "toys have no ability to learn, so they are bound to predefined actions and speech . . . [and] there is little evidence of haptic design" (p. 180). He recommends that more haptic experiences should be promoted by these toys because touch is a primary way that humans learn. In a review of a number of case studies of children's play with smart toys, he states that designers of such toys must realize play is a more complex concept than many designers have realized. He gives a number of suggestions for improving these toys to make the interfaces more natural. Kafai (2006) suggests that technology-augmented toys should have possibilities for encouraging all types of play—practice, pretense, and games. These various aspects of play are especially relevant for the affordance of challenge because flexibility of response is a component of challenge. Thus, the more varieties of play promoted by the toy, the more likely the toy will engage children's interest and motivation. In a discussion of learning through play, Anderson (2014) stresses the role of embodied cognition. He suggests that designers of technology-augmented play and learning devices should encourage playful interactions, support self-directed learning, allow for self-correction, and record and respond to data collected, but also that they should make learning tangible. He states, "nearly everything is experienced with and through our bodies . . . through physical interactions with the world around us and via our various senses . . . we should strive for manipulatives and environments that encourage embodied learning" (p. 131). Anderson gives some examples of such designs, including "Motion Math," "Sifteo Cubes," and "Game Desk," all of which incorporate aspects of embodied cognition.

Some suggestions for toy developers and marketers are the following:

- Technology-augmentation in toy product development should be used for the purpose of enhancing all areas of children's development in order to encourage their versatility and resilience.
- Research on the dynamic interactions of social, emotional, moral, and cognitive development and technology-augmented toy products should be financially supported by toy product developers.

Suggestions for Developers and Marketers of Digital Games

Most commercial digital games, excluding many open-source titles, are designed to make money and any realistic suggestion would need to account for the financial impact. If typical suggestions such as reducing violence in digital games were implemented, the result may not only affect how play is experienced, but there may be significant effects on other human facets of life, for example moral development. However, the issue of violence in games is very complex, having substantial financial and legal implications. Perhaps better suggestions for game developers and marketers should focus on the representation modes and affordances of these games, in an effort to make them "better" for children and young adults. "Better" in this case is not simply higher entertainment value, but a superior game would try to also attend to the player as a human being and the game itself as a useful play activity. Some games already have features that attend to the human player. For example the online game Guild Wars™ has a feature that informs the player about the amount of time spent playing in the current session, and after a certain amount of time, the system suggests that the player "take a break." Features like this are separate from, for example, a game developer making a more comfortable controller so that players can play for a longer time.

Attending to the humanity of the player might lead game developers to put more focus on increasing the *enactive* mode of the game. That is, advances in virtual reality may allow game developers and marketers to see the benefits of building games that include more body movement. In terms of affordances, more emphasis could be placed on increasing challenge and accessibility. Game developers could design games that are less repetitive, requiring novel interaction from the user in an effort to increase challenge. Similarly, games could be designed to encourage more interaction with others, preferably real interaction with a shared physical space. There are games that already implement some of these suggestions such as some titles from the Wii system, but this is not the reality in most cases.

According to Lauwaert (2007), there are also some constraints on creativity and initiation of possibilities even in games such as SimCity™ (created by Will Wright), which was designed to be open to possibilities. Wright compared his game to play with railroad sets and dollhouses and considered it another form of toy.

However, because it is "an airtight software system" (p. 207), the player must conform to the design of the game. The feedback mechanisms that are embedded in the game strongly shape the way players can use the game. Lauwaert suggests that this is one of the ways game play differs from play with construction toys or other playthings and notes that because game designers try to make the technology embedded in order to enable players to be immersed in the game rather than aware of the technology, this prevents the players from playing "out of the box."

In a recent review of video game research, however, Eichenbaum, Bavelier, and Green (2014) describe results of game play that show enhancement of perceptual, attentional, and cognitive skills. Some of this research has focused on assisting children with disabilities and older adults with cognitive impairments. They assert, "video games are neither intrinsically good nor intrinsically bad. Instead, the nature of their impact depends upon what users make of them" (p. 67). They conclude that their review of this research suggests that video games can serve a good purpose, especially for children with disabilities. Kahn (1999, 2004) has reported on an interactive computer puzzles game called ToonTalk that acts as a tutor to teach children how to design programs. The puzzles gradually introduce programming constructs and techniques within a playful context. This author stresses that programming can be learned by both children and adults in a playful way by doing these puzzles.

Wolpaw et al. (2000), in a summary of an international meeting on brain-computer interface technology, have asserted that, in regard to games, "The affordances of the features in the game seem to be most important for the player" (p. 1). They question whether specific learning goals are met in games because it may be what the players really learn is "computer game literacy." This view has some support from Linderoth, Lindström, and Alexandersson (2004), who videotaped elementary age children's play with four games (a car building game, a hospital manager game, a noble family reputation building game, and an avatar battle game). They concluded that the children were able to design ways "to communicate the affordances of different game features to each other . . . [and] treated the game itself as an object of learning" (p. 164) rather than learning other concepts to apply outside of the game situation. In 2000, Chidambaram and Zigurs (2000) predicted that there were many games being developed for the internet and they pointed out that businesses were developing many online games that "take advantage of the Web's unique nature for playing games and paying for them" (p. 145). Separating out the business motivations for offering games to children and adolescents from other motivational sources is not easy, and thus, designers of such games have a role to play in evaluating both the potentially positive and negative developmental effects of online game play.

In the light of the varied views held about digital games, suggestions for game designers include the following:

- More enactive mode, higher challenge, and increased accessibility should be the rule for game design rather than the exception.
- Research on the dynamic interactions of social, emotional, moral, and cognitive development and digital games should be financially supported by game designers and marketers.

Suggestions for Developers and Marketers of Online Play Environments

Similar to the suggestions for digital games, developers and marketers of online play environments should consider improving their products in terms of the enactive representations, and challenge and accessibility affordances. Recent developments in both augmented and virtual reality systems may help in terms of the enactive mode. One example of the shift to this mindset is the acquisition of Oculus VR, maker of the Oculus Rift Virtual Reality headset, by Facebook. While the purchase is more than likely a financial decision, the result may alter the future direction of product development because of the attention paid to the enactive mode. Recent developments in virtual reality systems may help in terms of the enactive mode. That is, those who manage Facebook may be searching for more and better ways to enrich social interaction online, and one solution is to engage more senses and thus integrate the "whole" user into the virtual experience. The new sensory-rich experience will add value in terms of the enactive mode, and also it makes much financial sense in that users may find the experience appealing and the increase in new members coupled with the retention of the old members will be financially beneficial to Facebook.

Increasing challenge is a primary goal of many online play environments. In most cases, developers and marketers seek to build systems where users have a wide variety of tasks and options. The aim is to prevent users from feeling that the system is repetitive or that there are too few options for interaction. Suggestions in this area would be to continue developing ways to increase the nonrepetitive interactions among users. Similarly, accessibility is a major focus of many online play environments, because the systems depend on users interacting, albeit not in the same physical space. Developers should continue finding ways to connect individuals and removing the barriers that prevent or limit communication. Aside from technical or technological challenges, every effort must be made to ensure equal participation by diverse groups to ensure maximum accessibility. For example, systems should be designed to eliminate biases, such as gender and ethnicity, and minimize the effects of the "inauthentic person" (Bergen & Davis, 2011), the latter being a primary concern in terms of the potential to create caustic environments that users then avoid.

Developers and marketers of online play environments could also pay more attention to the human person as they develop their systems. Granted, they benefit most when the individual is using their system for extended periods of time, but at some point the pervasiveness of the virtual world may begin to have negative consequences in the real world. At this point, the individual may be forced to withdraw from the service and the loss of membership may have financial consequences for the service. Ideally online play environments would seek to promote balance in their members. This is admittedly very difficult when there are many systems and each is vying for as much attention from the user as it can get. Without changes, however, the current deluge of Twitter Tweets, Facebook updates, and Instagram posts will likely increase to the point where it negatively affects users, who will begin to abandon at least a subset of these systems. As is the case with technology-augmented toys, some online game developers are attempting to incorporate features that promote positive child and adolescent development. For example, Hsu and Lu (2003) have discussed an online game experience (TAM) that is designed to provide "a flow experience" that encourages attention, curiosity, and intrinsic interest. They state that "designers should keep users in a flow state" (p. 863).

Those who are involved in the development and marketing of games are encouraged to be attentive to the pervasiveness of games and game mechanics. The interest in the beneficial aspects of game play for development and learning comes not only from the game developers, but also from educators. The attention, curiosity, and intrinsic interest that are part of this flow state is one aspect that makes game-based learning appealing. Van Eck (2006) describes this shift in perspective as "we have largely overcome the stigma that games are 'play' and thus the opposite of 'work'" (p. 17). The connections between play and work are sometimes perceived in contradictory terms. In reviewing responses from a survey that was part of the Pew Internet and American Life project, Anderson and Rainie (2012) describe both positive and negative perceptions of using game mechanics to drive action for various purposes. Positive perceptions included the belief that "gamification will be an increasingly common aspect of everyday digital activities" (p. 3). Negative perceptions reported concerned the ongoing trend of gamification as being possibly "used for behavioral manipulation" (p. 5). The degree to which game concepts can be co-opted for specific purposes are innumerable and include those that appear to have altruistic purposes, such as the gamified educational endeavors of Khan Academy, or those that have recruiting purposes such as the games developed as a military recruiting tool for the U.S. Army (http://www.americasarmy.com/). Although these two examples are overt in their purposes, it is also possible that other games are either intentionally or unintentionally developed with less overt purposes.

In many cases, online games inherently facilitate the formation of virtual communities, which encourages social interaction within the virtual environment. Real-world concepts such as "social capital" appear to exist within this space, for example Steinkuehler and Williams (2006) argued that massively multiplayer online games (MMO) "are new (albeit virtual) 'third places' for informal sociability that are particularly well suited to the formation of bridging social capital" (p. 903). While these concepts seem inherent to the medium, developers could pay special attention to designing systems that either enable or enhance a game's ability to act as a beneficial social tool. Such actions would be fully supported by research examining the social aims that online games can serve. To that end, Trepte et al. (2012) recommended that there should be ways for encouraging "physical and social proximity as well as familiarity in gaming" (p. 838). They state that this is one way to increase "social capital" and lessen "the potential negative effects of online gaming by transforming games into an activity with a positive potential for offline friendships" (p. 838).

A recent study by the Pew Research Center (Hampton et al., 2014) investigated the concern that intensive social media interaction may lead to stress. These researchers reported that users did not report more stress due to time spent on these sites but did seem to find stressful much of the information that was communicated on the site. No matter which media they used (e.g., Pinterest, Facebook, Instagram, Twitter), the high users were more aware of stressful events occurring to friends or family. In particular younger users and females were more likely to report awareness of stressful events in the lives of their contacts. Thus, the researchers concluded that high stress levels were not directly the result of the media use but were related to the messages that users were receiving. Because of the less subtle messages that younger children and adolescents may send on these media, it may be that their stress from use may be greater. The reports of bullying would suggest that the overt stressful messages can be harmful; however, more research is needed before definite conclusions about stress relationships to these media can be confirmed. In any event, the "playfulness" of some of these media may be questionable.

Thus, suggestions for marketers of online play environments include the following:

- Some systems should be designed that foster social and emotional health and moral and cognitive complexity rather than requiring only instantaneous, shallow, and potentially stressful interactions.
- Research on the dynamic interactions of social, emotional, moral, and cognitive development and various online play environments should be financially supported by online game and communication developers.

Suggestions for Community Stakeholders

The future of play and the future of humans in the larger society are not just issues for parents, educators, toy product designers, or digital game and online play environment designers. They are crucial issues for many other stakeholders as well. For example, these activities raise issues for corporate entities, community organizations, government policy makers, and cultural values proponents. In particular organizations concerned about child and adolescent media use such as the American Academy of Pediatrics (2013) have made policy statements regarding the amount of time that children of various ages should be involved with technology-augmented devices. Another organization, the National Association for Education of Young Children, which focuses on issues related to children from birth to age 8, has a position statement done in collaboration with the Fred Rogers Center that conveys their advice about technology-augmented play experiences. For example, they suggest that, because children use technology in ways that are similar to their other play experiences, "young children need opportunities to explore technology and interactive media in playful and creative ways" (NAEYC & Fred Rogers Center, 2012, p. 7).

Most of the questions about how various types of technology-augmented play will influence future society have not even been identified, much less discussed in depth. Nevertheless, there are many questions about extremes in technology-augmented play that may have future societal implications. For example, hacking digital and online games is generally perceived as an example of playfulness with minimum consequences, but the hacking of corporation or government sites differs in moral quality. Similarly, designing a playful program that engages many young people online may have no lasting societal implications while designing a playful program containing racial, gender, sexual, or religious biases that may be harmful to others is questionable. Sutton-Smith (1998) has written about the "out of bounds" types of play that also are part of human experience but that have no educational or developmental benefits although they may be approved as "festive" parts of a particular culture. These extreme types of playful behaviors do not foster the social, emotional, moral, or cognitive development of children and adolescents. Concern about technology and its effect on development has been voiced by many organizations; for example, a Centers for Disease Control whitepaper by Kachur et al. (2013) outlines concerns and presents suggestions regarding adolescents, technology, and sexual health. Levin (2013) suggests working at the societal level for appropriate laws and policies and at the educational level for media literacy education.

Because of the wide-ranging and pervasive influence of technology-augmented play materials, the potential for harm from technology-augmented out-of-bounds play is great, and therefore, unanticipated effects of this type of play should be monitored by community stakeholders and policies should be designed to address such issues.

Thus, suggestions for community stakeholders include the following:

- Policies that promote developmentally rich play in a variety of environments, including outdoor venues, should be supported by communities.
- Practices that promote potentially harmful effects on young persons should be monitored and policies to promote beneficial effects should be advocated.
- Research on the social, emotional, moral, and cognitive effects of various play venues should be supported by community agencies, foundations, and governmental organizations.

Recommendations for Parents and Educators

Although all of the stakeholders previously discussed have a role to play in ensuring that the social, emotional, moral, and cognitive developmental effects of technology-augmented play materials are positively focused, there will continue to be problematic issues that must be addressed by parents and educators. Because they are most aware of the possibilities of dynamic system interactions, ultimately, their role in protecting the experiences that will result in optimal brain maturation and enriching playful experiences for young children, older children, and adolescents also will depend on their encouragement of play that leads to versatility and resilience for future generations. How parents should guide their children's use of internet resources is a problem throughout the world, as a study of this issue in Jordan indicates (Ihmeideh & Shawareb, 2014). These researchers found that parents with authoritative (as compared to authoritarian, permissive, and neglectful) parenting styles did act in ways that predicted how their children used the internet. They suggest that parenting programs, school policies, and the designers of media should collaborate to assist parents in knowing how to manage their children's pervasive internet use. Robb and Lauricella (2014) also have advice for educators about their use of technology-augmented devices in the classroom and this advice is good advice for parents. They state that decisions about what devices to make available to children should be based on the "developmental level, interests, abilities, linguistic background, and needs of the children in their care" (p. 81).

For Infants and Young Children

One of the best ways for parents and educators to know what is most important in regard to young children's play is to recall the types of play that they found most enjoyable when they were children. Often the most important characteristics adults remember about their play are the powerful feeling of control over their own experiences (i.e., being "in charge") and the challenges they met by creatively affecting their play environment (i.e., exploring possibilities). No matter what type of play materials are involved, the best play gives young persons a feeling of control over their world. At later ages, this feeling can translate into versatile thinking in the face of problems and resilient responses to solving such problems. While there are many ways that rich play experiences for infants and young children can be promoted by parents and educators, here are a few of the most useful suggestions:

- Young children should be afforded a wide variety of play experiences because this will enable them to build a more dense and connected brain.
- This play variety should extend to outdoor space as well as indoor space because the natural world must be part of their humanness.
- They should engage in face-to-face positive interactions in play with adults and with peers to ensure sufficient enactive mode (embodied) cognition.
- They should have sufficient amounts of time for play in which their own choices of activities and experiences are available.
- The play materials should include both traditional and technology-augmented ones and a balance should be maintained.
- The affordances of the play materials should be evaluated and ones with various levels of transparency, creativity, and accessibility should be provided.
- Technology-augmented toys and virtual play materials should not become substitutes for human interactions.
- Young children's social interactions should be varied in terms of people and perspectives.
- Adults should act as role models by demonstrating that they are not tied to technology-augmented interactions but also model face-to-face social skills.

For Older Children and Adolescents

As the young person's world expands, parents and teachers should signal their confidence in the versatility and resilience that the children have gained through their earlier elaborated play experiences. They should state that they expect responsible decision making about the amount of time devoted to technology-augmented play in relation to other types of play activity and give the support that is needed to assure that some balance is maintained.

Suggestions for this age level include:

- All of the aforementioned recommendations continue to apply.
- Discussions of technology-augmented play and its values or problems should be part of family interactions and school projects.
- Technology-augmented play should be permitted according to the child's interests but it is not necessary to encourage them strongly to use technology.
- The types of social, emotional, moral, and cognitive messages that are provided by various types of technology-augmented play should be part of everyday adult-child discussions, especially in the adolescent years.

- Self-regulations skills should be encouraged so that young people control their technology-augmented play rather than having it control them.
- Discussions of future abilities and personal characteristics needed for responsible and fulfilling adult life that do and do not depend on technology-augmented skills should be part of parent and educator interactions with adolescents.
- Adults should engage in some forms of joint play with their children and explain how such play supports their own social, emotional, moral, and cognitive development.

For All Age Levels

One of the best ways to assure that young people gain versatility and resilience from their play is by having adults in their environment who value play and have a playful attitude throughout life.

Thus, this suggestion:

- The value of a wide range of play experiences as being essential for all humans should be recognized and promoted.

The Future of Play and of Human Existence

In a wide-ranging book called *The Future of Mind*, Kaku (2014) discusses the "evolving" brain, the development of the "artificial" mind (i.e., computer mind) and the very wide range of possible futures the human race may encounter. He is open to all of these possibilities but after reviewing the potentially amazing and useful as well as the problematic changes that may occur, he concludes by saying, "it is up to us to adopt a new vision of the future that incorporates all the best ideas. To me, the ultimate source of wisdom in this respect comes from vigorous democratic debate" (p. 322).

Play is a basic part of the human experience and it will continue to be exhibited in many forms for many generations to come. Because of the rapidity of technological change, it is not possible to predict what the playthings of the future will be. For those who are concerned about optimum child and adolescent brain, social, emotional, moral, and cognitive development, however, the challenge will be to keep in mind the important features of play that have contributed to human evolutionary progress and to evaluate changing technology-augmented play within the perspectives that have been discussed. There is no question that playful humans who maintain their versatility and resilience throughout life will be able to find fulfillment in the future, whatever that may be. Thus, it is important to engage in the debate and make the future human-technology interface a playful and life-enhancing process!

FIGURE 6.1 I like to create my own songs.

FIGURE 6.2 My practice play for the real ball game is important.

FIGURE 6.3 I'm immersed in my reading world.

FIGURE 6.4 Having fun with puppy play and music play.

Activities and Questions for Discussion

1. Analyze the play of the three children of the Challenge/Smarter family and make suggestions for what the parents should do to promote their children's play in ways that will enhance their versatility, resilience, and adult success in the future society.
2. Imagine you are interviewing a toy products designer and list five questions you would ask that person about toy design and issues of future relevance. Suggest three research study plans that would gather information about the effects of toy products on the versatility and resilience of future children.
3. Review 10 digital games or online play environments and evaluate them in terms of their interest to male and female older children or adolescents, the social, emotional, moral and cognitive processes that they may promote, and the ways they might increase the versatility and resilience of the players. Give some guidelines for their use that would promote positive developmental outcomes from such play.

References

Allen, M. (2004). Tangible interfaces in smart toys. In J. Goldstein, D. Buckingham, G. Brougere (Eds.), *Toys, games, and media* (pp. 179–194). Mahwah, NJ: Erlbaum.

American Academy of Pediatrics. (2013). Children, adolescents, and the media. *Pediatrics, 132*(5), 958–961.

Anderson, J., & Rainie, L. (2012). The future of gamification. Available at: http://www. pewinternet.org/2012/05/18/the-future-of-gamification/

Anderson, S.P. (2014). Learning and thinking with things. In J. Follett (Ed.), *Designing for emerging technologies; UX for genomics, robotics, and the internet of things* (pp. 112–138). Sebastopol, CA: O'Reilly Media, Inc.

Bergen, D., & Davis, D. (2011). Influences of technology-related playful activity and thought on moral development. *American Journal of Play, 4*(1), 80–99.

Chidambaram, L. & Zigurs, I. (Eds.). (2000). *Our virtual world: The transformation of work, play and life via technology.* IGI Global.

Druin, A. (2009). *Mobile technology for children: Designing for interaction and learning.* Morgan Kaufmann.

Druin, A. (2010). Children as codesigners of new technologies: Valuing the imagination to transform what is possible. *New Directions for Youth Development, 128*, 35–43.

Druin, A., & Hendler, J.A. (Eds.). (2000). *Robots for kids: exploring new technologies for learning.* Morgan Kaufmann.

Eichenbaum, A., Bavelier, D., & Green, C.S. (2014). Video games: Play that can do serious good. *American Journal of Play, 7*(1), 50–69.

Ellis, M. J. (1998). Play and the origin of the species. In D. Bergen (Ed.), *Readings from play as a learning medium* (pp. 29–31). Olney, MD: ACEI.

Hampton, K. N., Rainie, L., Lu, W., Shin, I., & Purcell, K. (2014). Social media and the cost of caring. *Pew Research Center,* Washington, DC. Available at: http://www.pewinternet. org/2015/01/15/social-media-and-stress/

Hsu, C. & Lu, H. (2003). Why do people play on-line games? An extended TAM with social influences and flow experience. *Information & Management, 41*, 853–868.

Ihmeideh, F.M., & Shawareb, A.A. (2014). The association between internet parenting styles and children's use of the internet at home. *Journal of Research in Childhood Education, 28*(4), 411–425.

Kachur, R., Mesnick, J., Liddon, N., Kapsimalis, C., Habel, M., David-Ferdon, C., . . . Schindelar, J. (2013). *Adolescents, technology and reducing risk for HIV, STDs and pregnancy.* Atlanta, GA: Centers for Disease Control and Prevention.

Kafai, Y. (2006). Play and technology: Revised realities and potential perspectives. In D.P. Fromberg & D. Bergen (Eds.). *Play from birth to twelve: Contexts, perspectives, and meanings* (2nd ed., pp. 207–214). New York: Routledge.

Kahn, K.A. (1999). *Computer game to teach programming.* Proceedings of the National Educational Computing Conference.

Kahn, K. (2004). Toontalk-steps towards ideal computer-based learning environments. In M. Tokoro & L. Steels (Eds.), *A learning zone of one's own: Sharing representations and flow in collaborative learning environments* (pp. 253–270). Amsterdam: IOS Press.

Kaku, M. (2014). *The future of the mind: The scientific quest to understand, enhance, and empower the mind.* New York: Doubleday.

Kudrowitz, B. (2014). Emerging technology and toy design. In J. Follett (Ed.), *Designing for emerging technologies; UX for genomics, robotics, and the internet of things* (pp. 237–255). Sebastopol, CA: O'Reilly Media, Inc.

Lauwaert, M. (2007). Challenge everything: Construction play in Will Wright's SIMCITY. *Games and Culture, 2*(194).

Levin, D. (2013). *Beyond remote controlled childhood: Teaching young children in the media age.* Washington, DC: National Association for the Education of Young Children.

Linderoth, J., Lindström, B., & Alexandersson, M. (2004). Learning with computer games. In J. Goldstein, D. Buckingham, G. Brougere (Eds.), *Toys, games, and media* (pp. 157–176). Mahwah, NJ: Erlbaum.

Luckin, R., Connolly, D., Plowman, L., & Airey, S. (2003). Children's interactions with interactive toy technology. *Journal of Computer Assisted Learning, 19*(1), 1–12.

Lund, H. H., Klitbo, T., & Jessen, C. (2005). Playware technology for physically activating play. *Artificial life and Robotics, 9*(4), 165–174.

Lund, H.H., & Marti, P. (2009). Designing modular robotic playware. *Robot and Human Interactive Communication, 2009. RO-MAN 2009. The 18th IEEE International Symposium* (pp. 115–121).

National Association for the Education of Young Children & Fred Rogers Center for Early Learning and Children's Media at Saint Vincent College. (2012). *Technology and interactive media as tools in early childhood programs serving children from birth through age 8.* Washington, DC: NAEYC; Latrobe, PA: Fred Rogers Center for Early Learning and Children's Media at Saint Vincent College.

Resnick, M. (2006). Computer as paintbush: Technology, play, and the creative society. In Singer, D.G., Golinkoff, R.M., & Hirsh-Pasek, K. (Eds.), *Play = Learning: How play motivates and enhances children's cognitive and social-emotional growth.* New York: Oxford University Press.

Robb, M.B., & Lauricella, A.R. (2014). Connecting child development and technology: What we know and what it means. In C. Donohue (Ed.), *Technology and digital media in the early years: Tools for teaching and learning* (pp. 70–85). Washington, DC: NAEYC.

Smith, P. K. (2007). Evolutionary foundations and functions of play: An overview. In A. Goncu & S. Gaskins (Eds.), *Play and development: Evolutionary, sociocultural, and functional perspectives* (pp. 21–49). New York: Lawrence Erlbaum.

Steenbeek, H., van der Aalsvoort, D., & van Geert, P. (2014). Collaborative play in young children as a complex dynamic system: Revealing gender related differences. *Nonlinear Dynamics, Psychology, and Life Sciences, 18*(3), 251–276.

Steenbeek, H., & van Geert, P. (2005). A dynamic systems model of dyadic interaction during play of two children. *European Journal of Developmental Psychology, 2*, 105–145.

Steinkuehler, C.A., & Williams, D. (2006). Where everybody knows your (screen) name: Online games as "Third Places." *Journal of Computer-Mediated Communication, 11*(4), 885–909.

Sutton-Smith, B. (1998). The struggle between sacred play and festive play. In D. Bergen (Ed.), *Readings from play as a medium for learning and development* (pp. 32–34). Olney, MD: ACEI.

Thelen, E., & Smith, L.B. (1994). *A dynamic systems approach to the development of cognition and action.* Boston: MIT Press.

Trepte, S., Reinecke, L., & Juechems, K. (2012). The social side of gaming: How playing online computer games creates online and offline social support. *Computers in Human Behavior, 28*(3), 832–839.

Van Eck, R. (2006). Game-based learning: It's not just the digital natives who are restless. *EDUCAUSE Review, 41*(4), 16–30.

Wolpaw, J.R., Birbaumer, N., Heetderks, W.J., McFarland, D.J. McFarland, Hunter Peck-ham, P., ...Vaughan, T.M. (2000). Brain-computer interface technology: A review of the first international meeting. *IEE Transactions on Rehabilitation Engineering, 8*(2), 164–173.

EPILOGUE

Wisdom of the Velveteen Rabbit

In one of the early books that the first author wrote (Bergen, 1998), she addressed issues related to the beginning phases of the movement to add technology-augmented qualities to many traditional play materials, such as stuffed toys and dolls that laughed or said phrases when buttons were pressed, blocks and other construction materials that had electronic components, and cars and trucks that were operated with battery-embedded devices. In her remarks, she quoted from Williams-Bianco's (1926, pp. 16–17) story of the *Velveteen Rabbit* on the issue of what makes something "real." In that story the old rocking horse gives advice to the stuffed rabbit, saying that children quickly forget or discard the toys that "break easily" or "have to be carefully kept." He asserts that the toys that are really loved are the ones who stay with a child so long that their fancy qualities have been "loved off" and it is only then that they become "Real." And the horse asserts, that "once you are Real you can't be ugly, except to people who don't understand" (p. 17).

In response to Williams-Bianco's views, Bergen wrote the following comments in her book, which she believes continue to be true today:

> So how do we become real in a technological age?
>
> The same playful qualities that saved humans from the vagaries of primitive existence and that have brought us into this present complex society can help us to find and preserve our realness in the future ... When children engage in play, trying out practice skills, trying on pretend roles, trying to live by game rules, they can learn much about their authentic selves. By testing the limits of their abilities in the self-imposed activities of play, they can find out who they are and realize what they can become ... It is important that as children learn to individuate, classify, accept, and come to terms with socially identified realities, they don't lose the opportunity to "become real" in the process. ...

Play can provide a medium for linking technological learning and our self-knowledge-seeking. To adapt to the world of the next century, with its as yet unimagined human, scientific, and technological possibilities, we have to be able to think in "as if" and "what if" ways. In our concern about the possible negative effects of technology, I think we have often ignored its play and self-enhancement potential, which can help us in our search for realness. For example, computer networks are demonstrating that technology can connect the mind and heart and leave the irrelevant characteristics of the body—gender, physical appearance, race, handicaps—behind, thus opening up a new world of play and communication of "unencumbered" ideas and feelings. Play also serves as a medium for technological conquest, as the simulations that prepare adults for space flights demonstrate . . . In the same way that play provided a medium for invention in other centuries, it encourages the thinking and dreaming that are needed for survival now . . . A playful attitude toward life allows us to keep in touch with ourselves while we examine, accept, manipulate, and integrate our many realities. Once we learn to do that, we can even reframe and integrate the realities of our work with those of our play and experience the joyful "flow" that comes from this holistic authenticity. As we open ourselves up to the "as ifs" and "what ifs" in our futures, transform our work into play and our play into work as the need arises, and see beyond our props, roles, and appearances to embrace our realness—even those parts of us that are a bit worn and shabby—we will convey to children our knowledge that a life playfully and actively lived is worth the risk. We will know (as the Toys know) that "once you are Real, you can't be ugly, except to people who don't understand."

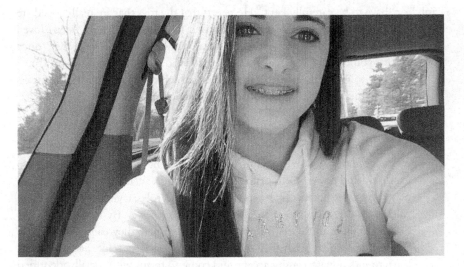

FIGURE 7 A Selfie!

References

Bergen, D. (Ed.). (1998). *Play as the medium for learning and development: A handbook of theory and practice*. Portsmouth, NH: Heinemann Educational Books.

Williams-Bianco, M. (1926). *The velveteen rabbit: or, How toys become real*. New York: Pioneer Drama Service, Inc.

GLOSSARY OF BRAIN AND NERVOUS SYSTEM TERMS

Brain Components

Amygdala. An almond-shaped mass of nuclei that form part of the gray matter in the front part of the temporal lobe; part of the limbic system; involved in processing and expressing emotions.

Basal ganglia. A group of structures deep in the cerebral hemispheres involved in inhibition of motor movements.

Brain stem. The section of the brain that includes the diencephalion (thalamus and hypothalamus), midbrain, and hindbrain.

Cerebellum. A structure in the hindbrain specialized for motor coordination; also plays a role in learning and memory.

Cerebrum. The rounded structure of the brain occupying most of the cranial cavity; divided into two hemispheres.

Corpus callosum. The fiber system that connects the two hemispheres of the cerebrum.

Cortex. The outer layer of the brain, containing four to six layers of cells.

Fissures. Deep clefts produced by folds of the cortex.

Forebrain. The portion of the brain that includes the cerebral hemispheres, basal ganglia, thalamus, amygdala, hippocampus, and septum.

Frontal lobe. The portion of the cortex that is in front of the central sulcus.

Gyri. Convolutions of the cortex in the cerebral hemispheres.

Hemisphere lateralization. Specialization of functions in the two cerebral hemispheres.

Hindbrain. The region of the brain that contains the cerebellum, medulla, pons, and fourth ventricle.

Hippocampus. A structure in the anterior medial region of the temporal lobe, involved in memory, learning, and emotions.

Hypothalamus. A structure below the thalamus, involved in behavior regulation (e.g., movement, feeding, sleeping, temperature, emotional expression, sexual activity, endocrine production).

Insula. A portion of the cortex folded deep within the lateral sulcus involved in consciousness, emotion regulation, perception, motor control, self-awareness, other cognitive functions, and interpersonal experience.

Limbic system. The neural systems on the inside wall of the cortex, surrounding the corpus callosum and brain stem, involved in learning, memory, and emotions.

Medulla. The portion of the hindbrain near the spinal cord; regulates reflexes and blood pressure.

Midbrain. The short segment between the forebrain and the hindbrain.

Occipital lobe. The regions of the cortex at the back of the head; site of visual perception.

Parietal lobe. The regions of the cortex lying beneath the parietal bone; site of motor and sensory perception.

Sulci. Small clefts produced by the folding of the cortex.

Temporal lobes. The regions of the cortex lying laterally on the sides of the head; site of language perception and speech.

Thalamus. The structure that relays visual, auditory, and sensory information to and from the cortex.

Ventricles. The cavities of the brain that contain cerebrospinal fluid.

Nervous System Components

Axon. The part of the neuron that transmits action potentials from the cell body to other neurons, muscles, and glands.

CNS. The central nervous system, including the brain and spinal cord.

Dendrites. The treelike structures of the neuron that receive information from the axons of other neurons.

Efferent nerves. Nerves that conduct impulses away from higher centers in the central nervous system toward muscles and glands.

Glia. The brain cells that provide support for the neurons and central nervous system.

Myelination. Formation of myelin coating on the axons; an index of brain maturation.

Neuron. The basic unit of the nervous system, functioning to store and transmit information (includes cell body, dendrites, axon).

Neurotransmitters. Chemicals released from synapses in response to action potentials; chemically transmit information from one neuron to another (e.g., cortisol, serotonin, dopamine).

Pruning. The process by which excess synapses are eliminated.

Synapse. The point where nerve cells make contact; junction between an axonal terminal and a dendrite of another cell.

Synaptogenesis. The process by which synapses multiply.

BRAIN DIAGRAMS

Brain Architecture

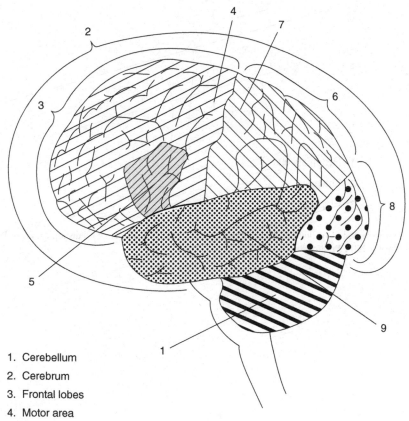

1. Cerebellum
2. Cerebrum
3. Frontal lobes
4. Motor area
5. Broca's area (language)
6. Parietal lobes
7. Sensory areas
8. Occipital lobes
9. Temporal lobes

Diagram adapted from *Brain Basics*, published by the National Institute of Neurological Disorders and Stroke; NIH Publication No.11–3440a

Inner Brain (Limbic System) Components

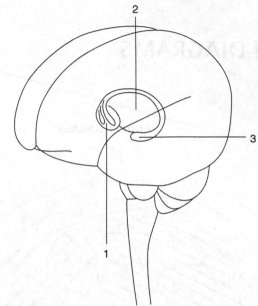

1. Hypothalamus
2. Thalamus
3. Hippocampus

Diagram adapted from *Brain Basics*, published by the National Institute of Neurological Disorders and Stroke; NIH Publication No.11–3440a

Brain Nervous System Components

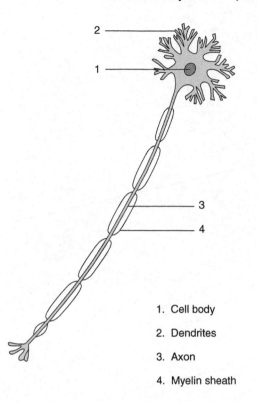

1. Cell body

2. Dendrites

3. Axon

4. Myelin sheath

Diagram adapted from *Brain Basics*, published by the National Institute of Neurological Disorders and Stroke; NIH Publication No.11–3440a

INDEX

mirror neurons 9, 99
Mishra, P. 107
mixed-reality 43, 46; continuum of 43
MMOs 66, 129
mobile gaming devices 63
More, T. 95
Morris, P. 100
Morris, S.R. 6
Mueller, P.A. 106
myelination 9, 99, 102–3

NAEYC 130
nanobots 97
Neary, L. 101
Nelson, C.A. 103
nervous system 8; definitions *see* glossary
neurons 9; neuronal network 9, 98
neurons, mirror 9, 99
Newcombe, N.S. 100
Newton, D. 105
Nineteen-Eighty-Four 96
Nintendo 63, 85
Nolan, J. 74

O'Brien, E.H. 106
Offermans, S. 42
on-line play environments 46, 67–70,
127–9
Opie, I. 13
Opie, P. 13
Oppenheimer, D.M. 106

Papert, S. 40
parents 2, 73, 110, 119, 131–3; videogame
responses of 80; interviews 80–6;
recommendations for 131–3
Parten, M. 14
Patchin, J.W. 42, 104
Patel, S.H. 80
PC games 63
Pellis, S.M. 7
Pempek, T.A. 69
Perry, B. 17
Peterson, J. 102
Petroff, J.G. 105
phones: cell 99; smart 123
physical, contexts 29, 42–3, 54–8; world
13, 15
Piaget, J. 7–8, 13, 14, 15, 18, 104, 106
Pinker, S. 99
Pinterest™ 88, 111
platform action games 65
Plato 6, 95

play 1, 102, 133; dynamics 122–3;
environments 29–36; interviews 80–9;
memories 30–7; outdoor 54, 131–2;
violent 101; in warfare 109
play development 5, 8, 12–13; 15, 98–100,
119, 123; construction 13; games 12–14,
104–5, 124, 128–9; practice 12, 124;
pretense 12, 99–101, 124
playfulness 120
Plowman, L. 38, 124
Polich, J. 78–80
Pope Edwards, C. 7
Poster, M. 19–20
PowerTouch™, study 76
pretense *see* play
pruning 9–10, 102

Rainie, L. 128
Rapoport, J. L. 11
recommendations 121–33
Reddy, S. 104
representation modes 29, 39, 44, 53, 57–8,
66, 68–9, 123, 125; *see* enactive; iconic;
symbolic
Rescue Heroes™, study 74–6
research 30–7; 73–80, 125, 127, 129–30
resilience 120–1, 133
Resnick, L. B. 40
Resnick, M. 105, 107, 123
Richert, R. 78
Rizzolatti, G. 9
Robb, M.B. 78, 131
Robinson, D.A. 15
robotics 54, 97, 102, 109, 123
Rodenbery, G. 96
Root-Bernstein, M.M. 13
Root-Bernstein, R.S. 13
Roskos, K. 15
Rosseti Language 77
Rousseau, J.J. 7
Rubin, K.H. 14
Russ, S.W. 15

Saby, J.N. 99
Salber, D. 41–2
SALT 77
sandbox games 65
Schonfeld, Z. 96
Schroer, J. 78
Scott, G. 110
Shapka, J. 76
Shawareb, A.A. 131
Shore, R. 10

simulation games 64
singularity 97
smartphones 63
Smilansky, S. 14
Smith, C.R. 99
Smith, L. B. 15, 16, 121–2
Smith, P.K. 120
social game play 69
social media 127–9
Sowell, P. 11
spatial knowledge, effects of virtual
    media on 106
stakeholders 2, 119
Steenbeck, H. 122–3
Steinkuehler, C.A. 129
Stephan, C. 38
Stevenson, O. 38
Strigens, D. 74
Sutton-Smith, B. 130
Swift, J. 96
symbolic representation 2, 6, 10, 58,
    66, 68–9
synaptogenesis 9–10, 102–3

tablets, electronic 63, 83, 99, 101–2, 123
technological innovation 6, 29–30
technology 1, 119; defining 19–20;
    interface 95; assistive 105; warfare
    108–9; designers 119
technology-augmented play 2, 8, 54, 57,
    73–4, 89–90, 98, 99, 101–10, 124, 130;
    effects 37–47; 84–6
television 102–3; violent 102
Thelen, E. 15, 16, 121–2
Thomas, R. 78
Thompson, R.A. 103
Tickle Me Elmo™ 55, 59
toys, traditional 43–7, 54; design 123–5;
    smart 124; technology-augmented 54–5,
    60–1
toy designers/developers 53, 110,
    123–5
transparency 40–1, 43, 58–61, 66–7, 68–9,
    74–6, 78, 101, 132
Trepte, S. 129

Utopia 96

Vandenberg, B. 14
Vanderven, K. 15, 21
van der Aalsvoort, D. 122–3
Van Eck, R. 128
van Geert, P. 122–3
van Geert, T. 16
Van Hise, J. 96
versatility 120–1, 133
video games 46, 54, 89, 105, 108; age levels
    34–6; research on 30–7, 78–80
violence, game 101, 125
virtual 2, contexts 29, 42–3, 54–5, 61;
    communities 128; continuum 43;
    experiences 104; interactions 104;
    play 69; reality 68; world 104, 128
Vondrachek, S. 74
Vygotsky, L. S. 7–8, 12, 13, 14

Wake, M. 104
Wartella, E. 37, 78
Washburn, S.L. 6
Waters, E. 104
Wayne, T. 104
We, Y. 96
Weber, D. 74
Weigel, D.J. 38
Whiting, B. 7
Wilks, T. 78
Williams, D. 129
Williams, E. 30
Williams-Bianco, M. 23, 141–2
Wilson, M. 15, 100
Wilson, T. 74
Wingfield, N. 105
Wolpaw, J.R. 126
Woodin, M. 10
Wooldridge, M.B. 76
World Future Society 96–7
World of Warcraft™ 108
Wortham, J. 103

Xbox™ 62, 83, 113

Zamyatin 96
Zhang, X. 78, 80
Zigurs, I. 126
Zimmerman, F.J. 102

CPSIA information can be obtained
at www.ICGtesting.com
Printed in the USA
LVOW03*1655221116

514094LV00013B/204/P